onder

Marish
Stay away
from
Vegas.
Chase love!

THE BEST OF WRITE BLOODY
ANTHOLOGY

ଓ

EDITED BY DERRICK C. BROWN

WRITE BLOODY PUBLISHING

WRITEBLOODY.COM

First edition.
ISBN: 978-1949342352

Cover Design by Hollis Duncan
Interior Layout by Winona León
Edited by Derrick C. Brown
Proofread by Wess Mongo Jolley

Type set in Impact, Blackout, and Bergamo.

Printed in the USA

Write Bloody Publishing
Los Angeles, CA

Support Independent Presses
writebloody.com

for Daniel McGinn, Jeffrey McDaniel,
and Kim Addonizio

THE BEST OF WRITE BLOODY ANTHOLOGY

NASHVILLE 2004–2008

LOS ANGELES 2008–2011

AUSTIN 2011-2015

HOLLYWOOD 2015-2020

WORDxWORD
FESTIVAL
2012
wxw12.org

6:00 PM
POETRY
SLAM
FINALS
W/ JON
SANDS
&
JEANANN
VERLEE

I CAN READ BOO
THE
WRIT
BLOO
BOOK

OFFIC

ownpoet

NASHVILLE

2004–2008

It is strange that this press has lasted twenty years. Especially because I didn't know what I was doing when I started it. I was a paratrooper, got out of the army, wasn't sure what to do. Fell in love with poetry in Long Beach and LA. The weirdos and creeps, the savants and the drunks, the sweeties and the dark ones. They took me in, and I loved them. I wanted to get better. Wanted to tour the world. Wanted to lift other talented writers up. Never been rich. Wasn't sure what the hell I was doing, but I just did it. Begged for advice. Asked insiders for tips. Saw other presses fall. Asked writers what sucked about their deals and tried to make it better. No board or oversight. Just a unique taste in poetry and design. I am a lucky person. Let's take a trip, which begins in Spring Hill, Tennessee. We sold about forty books that first year! Special love shout out to the talented authors who we launched who did not fit within these pages like Victor Infante, Lea Deschenes, Michael Roberts, Buzzy, Paul Maziar, Matty Byloos, Danny Sherrard, Paul Suntup, Jade Sylvan, Rebecca Bridge, Ernest Cline and more.

—DCB

KUROSAWA CHAMPAGNE

This poem was built after watching Kurosawa's Dreams and The Lady from Shanghai by Orson Welles. It is infused with a time I watched a lover have a nightmare and did not wake her. The word Will-o-the Wisp is where wisped came from. It means a ghostly light that appears over bogs or marshes. Ursula means little bear. Ursa Minor is the actual star, also meaning smaller bear. Little bear is an inside joke between me and my former German lover.

Tonight
your body shook,
hurling your nightmares
back to Cambodia.
Your nightgown wisped off
into Ursula Minor.

I was left here on earth feeling alone,
paranoid about the Rapture.

Tonight
I think it is safe to say we drank too much.
Must I apologize for the volume in my slobber?
Must I apologize for the best dance moves ever?
No.

Booze is my tuition to clown college.

I swung at your purse.
It was staring at me.

I asked you to sleep in the shape of a trench
so that I might know shelter.

I drew the word surrender in the mist of your breath, waving a white sheet
around your body.

In the morning, let me put on your make-up for you, loading your gems
        with mascara
        then I'll tell you the truth.
        I watched black ropes and tears ramble down your face.

Lady war paint.

A squad of tiny men rappelled down those snaking lines and you said,
"Thank you for releasing all those fuckers from my life."

You have a daily pill case.

There are no pills inside.
It holds the ashes of people who burned
the moment they saw you.
The cinema we built was to play the greats but we could never afford the power
so in the dark cinema
you painted pictures of Kurosawa.

I just stared at you like Orson Welles,
getting fat off your style.

You are a movie that keeps exploding.
You are Dante's fireplace.

We were so broke,
I'd pour tap water into your mouth,
burp against your lips
so you could have champagne.

You love champagne.

Sparring in the candlelight.

Listen—
the mathematical equivalent of a woman's beauty is directly relational
to the amount or degree
other women hate her.

You, dear, are hated.

Your boots are a soundtrack to adultery.
Thank God your feet fall in the rhythms of loyalty.

 If this kills me,
 slice me open julienne, uncurl my veins
 and fashion yourself a noose so I can hold you
 once more.

THE BEGINNING

Buddy Wakefield is one of the most talented writer/performers I have ever met. I remember telling him how the press I was on folded and so I made my own company so I could tour Germany with my books. His books were not pretty but his heart was huge and his skill was blade-sharp. I told him I could help him print for cheap and make the books look pro and he didn't have to do what I used to do, which was print at Kinkos and sell a chapbook for five bucks. I asked my pal and fellow poet Lea Deschenes to help me design the interiors and I asked the bassist from Cold War Kids, Maust, and a woodworker named Bugbee to help me design some cover magic. Bingham Barnes made posters and some pals at Kidmo helped me make a website. We all loved the same music: Joy Division, Minutemen, A Tribe Called Quest, The Smiths, Pinback, Cocteau Twins, Slint, Drive Like Jehu. All that fun stuff. I tried to make the book covers look like old dime store crime novels with a rock and roll twist. I remember asking Borders how to get my books into their stores. A very kind employee said, "You're going about this all wrong. You can't just call a store and say 'help.'" But that's exactly what I did. He told me he tried to do a small press long ago and felt for me and hooked me up with their buyers and we had our first minor distro deal. It felt incredible, and the company began to grow. The end of the second year we had sold over two thousand books.

—DCB

DANIEL McGINN

1000
BLACK
UMBRELLAS

a Write Bloody Book

POEMS BY

DANIEL McGINN

SELF PORTRAIT III

Look at me, Father,
place my face in your hands.
I do not want to be alone,
I am uncomfortable with strangers.

I have storms inside of me.

My feet are not efficient, Father
and I want to run.
I am not strong or gifted,
I am hobbled like a horse.

Help me.
My hands are hammers,
I crush what I touch.

My head is awash with voices.
I memorize words instinctively.

Here is my darkness, Father.
I have hidden it under a bushel.
Take it.

Take these crumpled bills,
I have fished them from my pocket.
I am a fool with money.

Your mysterious hand
has fallen on my neck
and I cannot lift myself.

The pillow has buried my face
and no one sleeps
at the end of the hall.

Bless me, Father, teach me to cry.
I learned the language of women
but I have not learned to cry like a man.

Allow me to sit quietly
at your passenger side.

I packed myself a suitcase.
I wait where you left me
in a house full of women.

BLOOD RIVER

After I died I dwelled in all of my dwellings
from all of my lives all at the same time.
When I turned my head I would be standing,
or crawling, or sitting in a different room,
my room that kept changing, all the time.

If I were to blink my walls would become
windows into all of my streets, all of my yards,
where all of my mothers, and all of my fathers
and all of my children could congregate.

See the leaves rise up from the ground
and retake their places in the arms of bare trees.
Smell the moisture in the air, everything that was
rained upon is steaming with sunshine
and everything smells so clean.

I close my eyes and watch light streaming down
between the branches of redwoods trees. I know
what these trees are saying like I know my own name.

I reach to touch your hand, your face, but you are
sitting by the side of my hospital bed. I wish I could
give you my physical heart, the one I was born with.

At first I hid my heart in a house I made of Lincoln logs.
Later I hid it in cupboard in a house where we made love,
and babies, and arguments but soon the house fell down
and the pieces were taken to the city dump. I almost died.

I placed my physical heart into the hands of all the people
I ever became but they fought with each other because
they all thought they owned my heart. The doctor had to
cut me open to repair my heart. Now I see—I never owned
any part of my body—it always belonged to you.

I have reached the end of my shelf life but I still taste
the blood beginning to flow through my arms and legs.
I no longer hear the blood river leaping over dams.

My spirit can clear the dams.
You and I are liquid glass
We are always falling we go on,
we will never break.

CRISTIN O'KEEFE APTOWICZ

NEW MILLENNIAL BADASS

Let me tell you something.
When you wake up in the morning,
take a shower, get dressed, go to work,
and the first thing you do is turn on
your computer and look at photos
of two hot, hard guys doing each other
in the mouth and bum, you are either
on the road to getting fired

or you are me.

Let me tell you something.
When that cute guy from tech comes down
to audit your computer for "illegal hardware"
and finds three fisting videos, a *Beginner's
Guide to BDSM*, and the complete trailer
for the film *Ejacula*, and all he can say is:
Well, everything looks to be in order...

then honey, you can be safe
in the assumption that you are
the resident badass.

That's right,
I'm my internet company's
dirty little secret.

I'm the porn girl.

Only one on the floor. Only one in the building.
Only one getting paid cash money
to write copy like:

> *Panting for Panties:*
> *Let us get you to the brink*
> *with photos of ladies wearing*
> *nothing but wet cotton!*

I am getting people to the brink all day long,
and I don't even have to be in the same country as them.

I'm the New Millennial Badass!

Call me up at two in the afternoon,
and I'll tell you the URL where you can watch
Paris Hilton fuck for free.

Break up with your boyfriend,
and I will have him inserted
into an all 'leather daddy' gay erotica story,
where his name will be
the online gloryhole flashpoint
for so many cock-tugging burly bear men
that when he finally goes home
to the girl he broke up with you to be with,
he'll cum HTML all over her Banana Republic
beige tweed skirt.

Oh *yes*.

I'm *that* girl.

I'm the trouble maker.
Piss me off, and guess whose head
will be photoshopped into a threesome
with Dick Cheney and George W. Bush?

I'm so hardcore, that compared to me,
Ron Jeremy is only double X.

I'm so hardcore, that my boss once yelled at me
for looking at CNN.com.

I'm so hardcore, that my computer dictionary
now accepts the words wetty, mangina,
and buttgasm: a word I created *myself*.

And I'm so hardcore, that I write poetry
during my lunch break.

And I'm so hardcore, that I am writing this poem
during my lunch break.

And I'm so hardcore, that I wish my lunch break
lasted all day, because I'd much rather be known
as the poet girl than the porn girl.

But I'm so hardcore, that I live in a country
that only spends 4 cents per citizen on the arts.

And I'm so hardcore, that when I tried to live
on my art alone, I had to budget myself
five pierogies a day just to pay rent.

And I'm so hardcore, that I took the first damn job
that came along and I lucked out with a rock 'n' roll job
where I watch naked people do naked things to each other
all day long and get paid for it.

But I am so hardcore, that I don't even care.

Because no matter how cool working for porn
seems at cocktail parties or at poetry readings,

the truth of the matter is I am being paid
not to write my own stuff for eight hours a day,
forty hours a week. And if that ain't the definition
of "anti-badass," I don't know what is.

But don't worry about me, honey,
because I've got a plan.

And not only that,
I've got a savings account
with a bitching interest rate.

And as soon as I suck off the porn industry
for as much money as I can, until my wallet drips
$100 bills down the insides of my thighs,
then I am kicking porn to the curb
and becoming the real New Millennial Badass.

Writing poetry all day, everyday.
Poetry so hardcore, that when it finally breaks
through that hot white wall of Academia,
all my readers are going to cum in unison
and only in iambic pentameter.

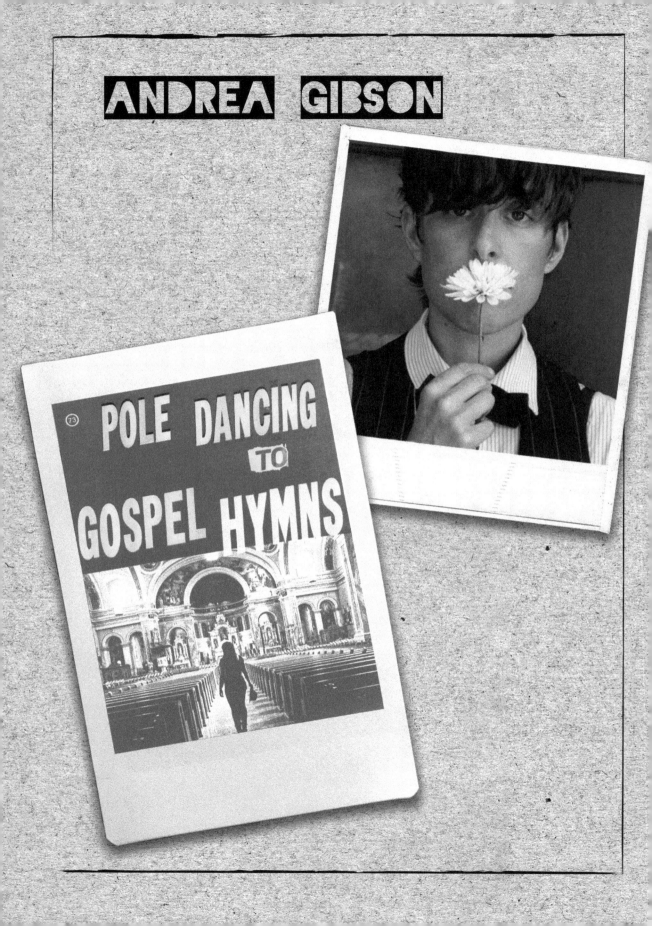

BIRTHDAY

for Jenn

At 12 years old I started bleeding with the moon
and began beating up boys who dreamed of becoming astronauts.
I fought with my knuckles white as dust,
and left bruises the shape of Salem.
There are things we know by heart.
And things we don't.

At 13 my friend Jen tried to teach me how to blow rings of smoke.
I'd watch the nicotine rising from her lips like fading halos,
but I could never make dying beautiful.

The sky didn't fill with colors the night I convinced myself
veins are kite strings you can only cut free.
I suppose I love this life,

in spite of my clenched fist.

I open my palm and my lifelines look like branches from an Aspen tree,
and there are songbirds perched on the tips of my fingers,

and I wonder if Beethoven held his breath
the first time his fingers touched the keys
the same way a soldier holds his breath
the first time his finger coaxes the trigger.
We all have different reasons for forgetting to breathe.

My lungs remember
the day my mother took my hand and placed it on her belly
and told me the symphony beneath was my baby sister's heartbeat.
and her lungs were taking shape

And I knew life would tremble
like the first tear on a prison guard's unturned cheek,
like a stumbling prayer on a dying man's lips,
like a vet holding a full bottle of whisky
as if it were an empty gun in a war zone…
just take me   just take me

Sometimes the scales themselves weigh far too much,
the heaviness of forever balancing blue sky with red blood.
We were all born on days when too many people died in terrible ways,
but you still have to call it a birthday.
You still have to fall for the prettiest girl on the playground at recess
and hope she knows you can hit a baseball
further than any boy in the whole third grade

and I've been running for home
through the windpipe of a man who sings
while his hands play washboard with a spoon
on a street corner in New Orleans
where every boarded-up window is still painted with the words
We're Coming Back
like a promise to the ocean
that we will always keep moving towards the music,
the way Basquiat slept in a cardboard box to be closer to the rain.

Beauty, catch me on your tongue.
Thunder, clap us open.
The pupils in our eyes were not born to hide beneath their desks. T
onight, lay us down to rest in the Arizona desert,
then wake us to wash the feet of pregnant women
who climbed across the border with their bellies aimed towards the sun.
I know a thousand things louder than a soldier's gun.

I know the heartbeat of his mother.

There is a boy writing poems in Central Park a
nd as he writes he moves
and his bones become the bars of Mandela's jail cell stretching apart,
and there are men playing chess in the December cold
who can't tell if the breath rising from the board
is their opponents' or their own,
and there's a woman on the stairwell of the subway
swearing she can hear Niagara Falls from her rooftop in Brooklyn,
and I'm remembering how Niagara Falls is a city overrun
with strip-malls and traffic and vendors
and one incredibly brave river that makes it all worth it.

I know this world is far from perfect.
I am not the type to mistake a streetlight for the moon.
I know our wounds are deep as the Atlantic.
But every ocean has a shoreline
and every shoreline has a tide
that is constantly returning
to wake the songbirds in our hands,
to wake the music in our bones,
to place one fearless kiss on the mouth of that new born river
that has to run through the center of our hearts
to find its way home.

Illustration by Anis Mojgani

This was a time of fascination. There were so many readings around the globe you could hit up and perform at if you wowed the promoters with

SAT

7

MUS

TICKE
AR
ONLY

IN THE WORLD

ly, Nettifee,
m, Boston),
Steve Abee

LOS ANGELES

CHEAP BEER AND CHEAP THRILLS!

TANKFARM 10900 LOS ALAMITOS BLVD., STE. 101, LOS ALAMITOS, CA 90720
CLOTHING TANKFARMCLOTHING.COM | WRITEBLOODY.COM

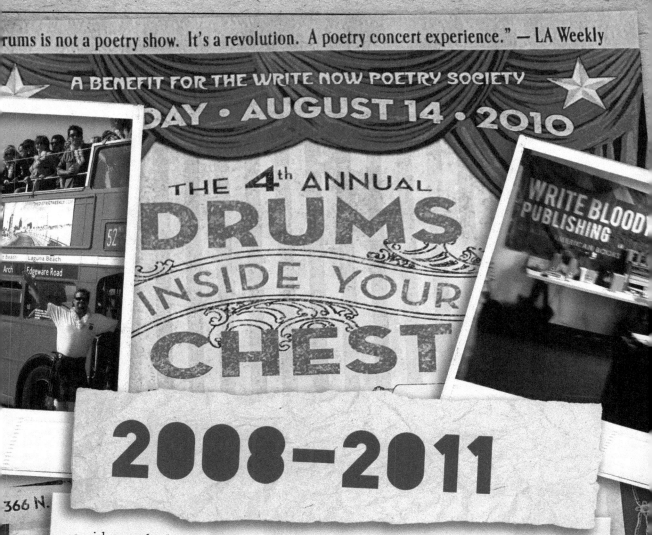

A BENEFIT FOR THE WRITE NOW POETRY SOCIETY

DAY • AUGUST 14 • 2010

THE 4th ANNUAL
DRUMS
INSIDE YOUR
CHEST

WRITE BLOODY PUBLISHING

2008-2011

a video or had someone vouch for you. I was living in Marina Del Rey on my second boat and was so lonely. I had just been fired from a TV writing job and was really scared. I had a boat loan to pay and all of Write Bloody's books were in storage. I would work out of a dark little 5 x 8 storage unit every day, shipping books, editing and designing things. It sucked hot butts. I moved the boat to a slip in Long Beach and found an office from an old record company called the Militia group that was vacant. They gave me 700 sq ft. for 300 bucks a month. It was awesome. When it was cold on my boat, I lived at Write Bloody. Showered in the office sink. Lived in the books. This was the time of the double-decker poetry bus parties, The Drums Inside Your Chest showcases, Write About Now shows in aquariums and art galleries, the Poetry at Sea ocean cruises I ran, and the Lightbulb Mouth Radio Hour weekly literary show. It was a golden time. I was trying to hustle to stay alive and just do poetry. Unless you're a teacher, it's pretty tricky.
DCB   —

BRENDAN CONSTANTINE

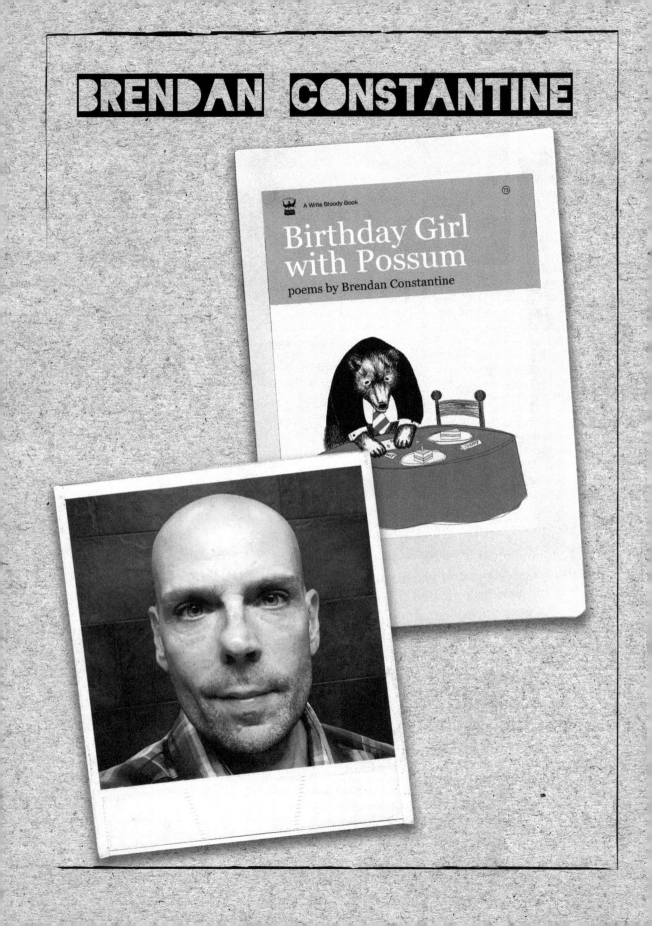

IN THE HOUSES OF THE NIGHT

In this island are certain glow wormes that shine in the night,
as doe ours…but give a greater light, so much that when the men
of the Iland goe any journeys in the night, they beare some of these
wormes made fast about their feet and head…By the light of these
also, the women worke in their houses in the night.
—Gonzalo Fernández de Oviedo y Valdés (1478 –1557)

In the houses of the night there are children who sleep, disfigured
by twilight, whose bodies mimic the dark margin of the landscape,
whose shadows terrify the children beside them. There are some
brave enough to face the wall, who laugh in their dreams, who ride
in boats small as leaves in a tub. Smaller.

There are men who take baths while smoking, while watching
the door, while talking to women. There are some who bathe
in total darkness, who walk wet to their beds, who stare
like horses, their eyes rimless, dark as tree water. They do not
dream. They would not survive it.

In the houses of the night there are dogs who speak like men,
there are birds who sing songs with words to them, garden
after garden of moths who mourn each closed flower, who die
of grief. There are spiders who make wreaths to catch them.
There are worms that call us into the ground like neon signs.

There are roads that remember canals, roads where the tar never
hardened & the blacktop gives like muscle, where the street lamps
tremble with the idling of sunken cars. The ants have gone mad
in their palaces. There are roads flooded with the ebon wings
of drone kings, roads that blow themselves out.

In the houses of the night there are women who whisper in closets,
who argue with mirrors, who talk easily to men in bathtubs.
There are some who bathe standing at a sink, who do it again,
who wash their bodies away. They do their sleeping like work.
They dream as a favor.

LETTER FROM MY VOICE

Dear Brian Stephen Ellis,
Stop Being Afraid Of The World.
          Sincerely,
          Your Voice

P.S. Stop blaming things on the insects.
Stop blaming things on the scathing eyes of men.
Stop blaming things on sand, and money, and the Sun.
Remember that your stomach is outside of your body
and your heart is just mystery waiting to become color.
You have tried to hide me in the paper sack of your intestines,
in the gambleshiver fist of your liver.
You have tried to hide me in your eyes,
the alarm clocks your mother built from snow globes and owl feathers.
Instead, I learned to scream from your tear-ducts.

I will abuse you until you claim me.
Have you seen the insides of your lungs lately?
They're covered in bruises.
I've been ripping nightmares out through your larynx
like tearing sheets of wool from your ventricles.
Now you cough up mobiles of twilight.

Brian — Your past is a motel;
every muscle in your body a room.
Hidden behind those doors are boys
you should have evicted long ago:
the teenager that let life
slip through knuckle heavy fingers,

the screaming adolescent that
punched himself in the night,
the grade school insomniac
with tear and snot scarred face,
the little boy who begged God
to take his imagination away
so he could finally sleep.
I never fit inside of those children.
Do not let the knife wound
of your caesarian birth chase you to the grave.

When you speak,
echo every gulp of oxygen
ancestor sacrificed to bring you to life.
When you speak, lift the ships of ghosts
in your veins into the air.
When you speak, make the bell
of your throat the champion of blisters.

Do not let the muscle shiners and the pollen-lipped
convince you that you are small.
Do not let the greedtarians and the cocksafe
look down their easy answers at you.
When you speak,
make the billows of your lungs
the mouth of the Atlantic.
When you speak, whip your crooked teeth
into a savage halo.
Bravery will never belong to the beautiful.
Remember that you are a conduit of the wind
and admit to me that you can fly.

I am the only thing you will ever truly own.
I am your voice.
And I am your only chance at freedom.

ELAINA M. ELLIS

WRITE ABOUT
AN EMPTY BIRDCAGE

Write about an empty birdcage. As in: write about your
ribcage after robbery. Use negative space to wind a song
from the place on the dresser where a music box isn't.
Write about the corners where the two of you used
to meet. Draw the intersections. Arrow to the side-
walk where her shoes aren't near yours. Write about

an empty birdcage. As in: write about a hinged-open
jaw that is neither sigh nor scream. Use this to signify
EXIT. Be sure to describe the teeth, the glint of metal
deep down in the molars, the smell of breath after lack
of water. Draw this mouth a thirsty and human portrait
of what it means to be used up. Write voice by writing

how it feels when it's painful to swallow. If you must
put noise in the scene, make it the sound of bird wings
flapping in a cardboard box. Take hope, and fold it
small as seed, then suck on it. Slow and selfish.
Write about an empty birdcage. Birdcage can read:
building, structure. Abandoned, or adorned. As in:

loop and tighten a vine of nostalgia around the room
you currently brick yourself into. Recreate the sweet
of jasmine, but mortar the door so it will not seep
through. Write about an empty birdcage. Replay us
the scene. As in: she presses her pale cheek against
the window, as he turns his pinstriped back, slow and

final. Again. She presses her pale cheek against the
window, as he turns his pinstriped back, slow and
final. Again. She presses her pale cheek against
the window, as he turns his pinstriped back, slow and
final. Write about an empty birdcage. Write about
the hinges. Describe them as dry knuckles. Write

how I became a moan.

KAREN FINNEYFROCK

A DETROIT TAROT

So the belly-dancing psychic says to me, one finger swirling toward the sky like an errant lightning rod, "Here's the deal, I'm pretty drunk, so I can't give you a full Tarot reading, but if you tell me your question, I'll pull a few cards."

She says this in her Detroit accent, so it sounds like she's negotiating knock-off time for the union crew at the auto plant. We are still awake at the end of the party, drinking wine from Yugoslavia out of a bottle shaped like a woman.

"My question," I say, holding the Tarot deck nervously like they are note cards for a debate speech, "is about love."

She looks at me like I have just made a smart-ass joke about the Pistons and she says, "Could you be a little more specific?"

"Like, will I find any soon?" I say, my voice growing twenty years younger in my throat, my voice growing a mermaid tail and a unicorn horn.

Christina (whose name is spelled on her Tarot business card with an X like "Xtina") lays down three cards, making the sound doctors make, "um hummm," she says, "well, now I know who you are. You construct men out of paper and glue and attach them to skies made of cardboard. You Mr. Potato them with the heads of high school teachers and the hearts of Brontë characters. You wrap string around muscle Voodoo dolls and hide them under your pillow..." and as dryly as I can muster it, I say, "Go on."

Placing three more cards below the first, she says "Ah ha, ten of wands, three of cups, you daily trip over fishing lines, cut yourself on the pages of mystery novels, you're always burning the house down to build castles out of pillows. You need to tie down the ropes of your dirigible, let the carnival wheels be still—there is one more thing I have to tell you, come closer, let me whisper...you treat intimacy like underwear, always hiding it under your skirt."

Xtina has turned my wine back into water, only now it contains salt. I'm about to say "Best to let sleeping cards lie," when she draws three more and yells "I know, I know what you need to do to find love!"

Christina, Cleopatra eyeliner and dark red lips, flowered headband and hoop earrings, Detroit racing through her past like a V8 engine, is leaning toward me, her breasts sitting in the cups of her bra like sleeping kittens, eyelids blinking too slow. She says, "Karen, this is what the cards are telling me, this is how you will find love," her fingers pinched together like she could pull raindrops out of the sky, she says, "when one of these men who turns you on is turning you on, tell him he is turning you on."

I always thought that when a drunk, belly-dancing, Tarot-psychic met me at a party and offered me the key to love like free tickets to a cabaret, I would wonder over its metaphorical complexity. But I knew, that night, a wise woman had offered me everything she gleaned from reading the stars in women's eyes. A powerful seer, brought up by the daughters of the automakers.

ROBBIE Q. TELFER

DEAR FLUFFY WALRUS,

I regret to tell you
my wife and I no longer require
your sooth-saying services.
Please dislodge yourself from our bath
and replace all the shampoo you've used—
that was never included.
I do not care if your bouncy curls
aide in your clairvoyance.
I do not care about you anymore,
Fluffy Walrus.

I hope your temperament will contain
largesse on par with your largeness
and you will not predict misfortune for us
out of malevolence, bruised feelings,
or famous and loathsome appetite.

We are a pain pair who
wish to no longer house
your fluffy walrus chicanery.

WHY WE ARE DIFFERENT

You like peppers.
I do not.

The girl you love is still alive.
You call her *home*. That is not her name-but
that is what you call her.

You're attracted to edge and class.
I like things that flow and look tattered.

I drop what I'm doing to pick up
your phone call.
You drop my phone calls to watch television,
or maybe masturbate,
or think about filling out a job application.
(I don't mean that to sound mean.)

You wake up early and I don't understand why.
Tears well in my eyes when I sit near lakes
and you don't understand why.

My voice cracks when I say certain things
and you don't notice.
You are in the background of a lot of pictures;
I notice.

You tell me I trust adjectives too much.
I tell you, you trust in not enough.

My comebacks are childlike, coyote-like, the wise fool.

I am messy. There are clothes all over my bathroom floor.

I haven't fully unpacked from a trip I've long
 since returned from.
You. You are tidy. Your underwear matches
 your mouth,
elastic and initialed.

You don't have many possessions;
 in a way, I admire it.
I keep everything,
even empty Sweet N' Low packets,
even a penis-shaped water bottle that leaks
and does not serve its purpose
as a water bottle.

You exercise...
that is funny.

Your kiss is uncertain.
I didn't know you were holding back on
 purpose. I thought your tonsils were shy.
I breathed on your lips.
You probably just thought I was out of shape
and panting.

I want to be a vampire.
That statement will frighten you.

You don't like my long hair and I know it.
I don't like your short hair, I told you.

I tell
much more
than you
ever
do.

You're better at games,
except for Red Rover; I am the best at that,
running full speed to break myself or someone
else.

You pick on me when I get poetic.
I pulled over to weep when you read the line,
"held each other like stolen televisions."

Once I read you a prayer,
you said it was weird.

You find no humor in breast feeding.
I say "that is funny" in place of actually
 laughing.

Your mom and dad.
My mom and dad.

When you get nervous, you pull away.
I get mad that traveling alone didn't make you
 nervous, like it would me.

I never went to prom.
You never had track marks.

I doubt you'd ever find a pale girl as pretty as I
 do,
though I will never like eggs.

When showering at night,
you do it before everyone is asleep as not to
 wake them up.
I get clean when I feel I need to. Water isn't
 THAT loud.

I don't know if you lie to me.
I am full of stupid hope.

We'll never be lovers,
we know this.
Still I want your heart in a penny pouch.

You love my midriff.
I'm thinking of aprons now....
and so the story goes.

When I ask what you like about me
you say I am fun.
It pisses me off.

You seldom ask what I like about you.
I never realized that, until now.
I like your quiet....
lavender bread in cellophane.

You said my eyes are sad
and it is really beautiful
how badly
I want happiness.

Sorry I never wore my red shoes. I was
 nervous.

"MIGHTY" MIKE McGEE

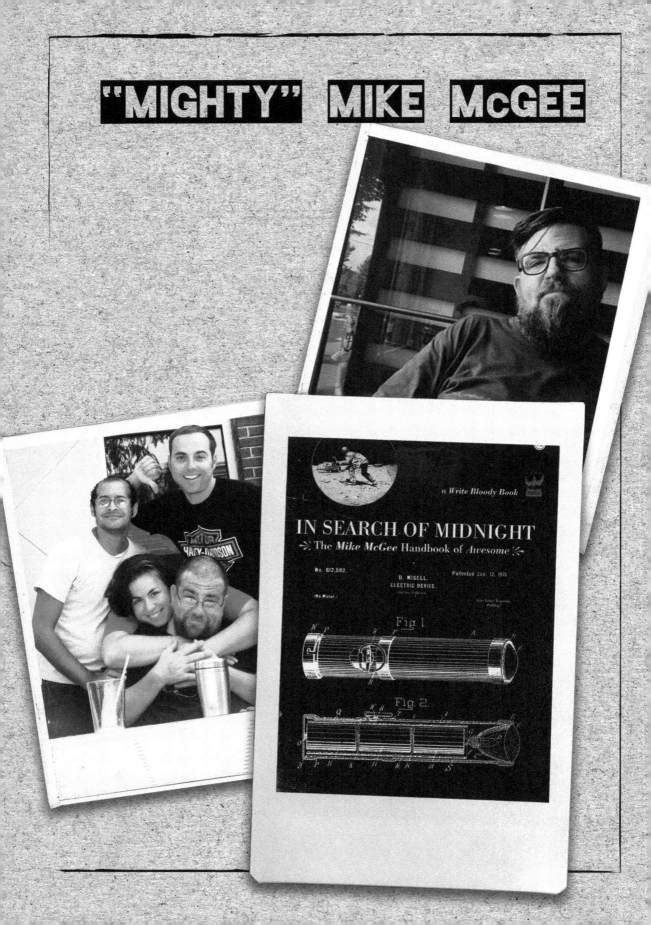

UNWIELDY

for Bobby Gibbs

If the only dangerous thing in a room is a person with a knife
and you can shrink yourself small enough
you will be able to stand on the tip of that knife

Only then can it not hurt you
but everything else in the room will

If you can enlarge yourself big enough
the only thing that can hurt you is the room itself

I know all of these sorts of people
There is no right way to be

It's just easier to be the one with the knife

SLEEPWALKER

I've been told it can be dangerous to wake up someone while they're sleepwalking. I believe it is far more disturbing to be awake, alone and motionless. Sleep has always felt like an incredible waste of time to me. Distance has always been a challenge to be covered, and if forever is a far-off town, and you live in said town, and you want me to live in said town with you, and if a town can be founded on a population of two, and the city centre is really just our bed, then we can sleepwalk without moving and say without speaking all that should be said, and if what needs to be said is worth saying, then I'm laying it on the line as we speak. Lady, I must keep moving toward you, especially when I'm weak. So I will walk and eat. Walk and sing. Walk and chew gum at the same time. I will walk and sleep with my eyes open to the hope and dream that this distance between us, akin to the distance between thunder and lightning, will some day be a little less frightening – once I can see you. Once I can take you by the hands and say that no matter how you lay your arms, they make a doorway to the only home that can heal the holes in this heart and head. Lady, I've been waiting for you for so long, I've learned to sleep standing in this lifeline, and I'm fine, but I can't stand sleeping knowing you stay up at night, afraid to dream the dreams of me in the starring role of the sleeper hit of the slumber. So this summer will pass and at long last, I will return to you, to lay your head across my chest. Just know that the best dreams I've ever had are the ones I have in store for us when we're both awake.

RYLER DUSTIN

HEAVY
LEAD
BIRDSONG

RYLER DUSTIN

$15.00

A write bloody

WHY WE DO NOT GO OUT

for Karen

Every week, my girlfriend and I
say that we should go hiking.
But we never do.

Last week our excuse was the cold.
The week before, it was the rain.

Today our excuse was that we got stoned.
The sky was so heavy around her apartment
that a wilderness grew inside of us,
waterfalls like white wrists,
forests with high dark trees
where insects beat dusk into the air
like a child rinsing her paintbrush
in a glass of water.

We were cartographers lost
in the country of ourselves.

When I leaned close to her chest,
I could hear the grasshoppers crooning,
the birds committing their vespers,
the last drowsy bees hanging like music notes,
carrying pollen from flower
to flower.

STEVE ABEE

ALLS OF FLOWERS

15.00

a Write Bloody Book

GAS

I.
Steve Abee is a gas station.
The Lord Jesus Christ is a gas station.
Jack Fris is a gas station.
Jack Kerouac is a gas station, too.
We are all gas stations, lonesome lovely gas stations
on the sandy skirt edge of the desert
dispensing starlight octane to each other as we move
from seashore to graveyard.

Time blows its bony nose into a Dixie cup
In the back of a Tijuana Greyhound.

The rain on the street smells like wet feathers.
The sky looks like a bowl of gray marbles.
The cloud kisses the rooftops.
Police cars, fire trucks, air raid horns, ambulances
wail sirens across the sky like John Coltrane
in a cacophonic meditation on love and suffering.
I taste the rain that falls from that horn.
It tastes blue.

That 3 am the boy drove his car into the wall
I could feel his breath dripping down the sidewalk
back to the sea.

Catherine Uribe is my wife. She speaks God.
Jerusalem, Jerusalem whisper the doorways.

II.
I am not a gas station. I have no fuel for you.
I am a mini mart. I fill the pre-dawn
nacho sauce need of the unwashed
and addicted.

The earth is in line for some meteoric hand jive.

When I lick your secrets the bombs begin to fall from your thighs.
It isn't polite to scream *fuckin' dick shit* in the middle of the night when
the whole house is asleep.

The shimmering tongue of disaster licks our wounds
Like a child licking the sugar dust from a Pixie Stick.
It is not the fire spiling from the windows
that causes me to be full of dear and dread,
but the trees who watch from the street
not understanding the orange tendrils of hatred and power.
It is not the sky that signifies endlessness
but your fingers pointing to the silence
That surrounds what you just said.

I turn into a plastic army man,
get lost in the backyard
and live on the nectar of the weeds.

III.
The Vexer responds with incredulity at being told how to write a poem.
The Vexer mocks the sounds of happiness that come from his belly.
The children tickle him to the green carpet. He cracks
up, turns   to dust.

IV.
The world will create a toilet that knows what is doing.
The world will stop at the stop lights and go at the go lights.
The world will stop fighting gravity, will accept
the truth of its own light.
The world will learn to whistle.
Our Gargantuan psychic underwear will be cleaned.
The time bomb within, full of high octane denial
will finally burst when all is created again.
Vamanos ala chingada.

Late at night the goldfish turns the light on in its aquarium,
sits on the rock, troubled by the mystery of water.
John Coltrane steps from his limousine at the Last Chance Gas.
The sun sets, he nods to the music in his hands.
Good-bye, Good-bye cry the golden horns of Jerusalem.

ROB STURMA

WHATEVER WE ARE NOT

Whatever we are not, this is what we are.
We are most definitely electric cattle prod dangerous.
We are toasters in bathtubs.
We are slap bass beautiful in a world of repetitive guitar solos.
We are habañero oil lingering on fingertips.
We may walk in circles most days, rapidly going nowhere,
but when kiss comes to love,
we have radar in our hips.

I have become your personal archeologist,
translating the Sanskrit written on the backs of your knees
into American Pop.
You have taught my inner quarterback the entire playbook
of sexy.
If you got a job as a gamma bomb,
I would gladly fling myself into your errant radiation,
even if I had to find a way to suppress the raging monster
inside me afterwards.
That's how deep this is.

Here's what we will never be:
Wal-Mart greeters.
Avon ladies.
Guidance counselors.

We tried being mediocre for a day,
but our alchemy changed us into meaty ogres instead,
and we ate twelve children. Dipped 'em in ranch.

We will never be cosmonauts. Too much gravity.
Our obvious poker tells keep us out of the Vegas circuit.
I am a jack o' lantern and you are my candle.
You, the pretty padlock; me, your secret locker combo.

I know the only labels you like are the ones on beer bottles,
and this is not what you think.
It's a lightning rod party.
It's a two-act playdate.
This is full-time employment in the blush factory.

We are not one-hit wonders. We are not negotiable.
We are heavyweight breathers,
conjuring a thousand secret smiles, and 999 perfect silences.
None of this is conjecture. I fell asleep and then I looked it all up.

So give it a name.
Give it a frame.
Hang it in the Louvre when no one's looking.

There are many ways to paint the canvas in between the
words "I" and "you."
This is just one of them—
but whatever this is not,
this is what we are.

JON SANDS

THE
NEW
CLEAN

a Write Bloody Book

"These are poems of a city's insistent romances and
our determination to root ourselves in its clutch, a
clutch that nurtures us while taking our breath away.
No one but Jon could have done this."
— PATRICIA SMITH

POEMS BY
JON SANDS

6:00 PM
POETRY
SLAM
FINALS
W/ JON
SANDS
&
JEANANN
VERLEE

DUSK

Me: Are you there?
Her: No.
Me: Your status says you're allergic to stars.
Her: Where do you live?
Me: Ohio.
Her: Are there bushes there?
Me: Like presidents?
Her: Like bushes.
Me: As many as I have fingers, right outside my window.
Her: What color are they?
Me: All the colors the sky makes, but mostly green.
Her: Are there hearts there?
Me: I hear them shuffling at night sometimes,
    but they sound just like wind on my chimes.
Her: So you never know.
Me: So I never know.
Her: Do you have one?
Me: I do.
Her: Where does it live?
Me: I feel like I've known you before.
Her: That makes one of us.
Me: You don't have a where?
Her: I'm a traveler.
Me: Am I dreaming right now?
Her: Can you feel your arms?
Me: There are definitely two strings
    attached at my shoulders that help me love.
Her: Can you feel *them*?
Me: I must be dreaming.
Her: Do you miss me?
Me: So I have known you.
Her: Do you
        miss me?
Me: Even when I don't know I'm doing it.
Her: If you could lie right now, would you?
Me: But I can't.
Her: I need to know.
Me: But I can't.
Her: I'll be all the way gone soon. Not just mostly.
Me: That's when I'll miss you most.
Her: You can find me.
Me: That's when I'll miss you most.

IDRIS GOODWIN

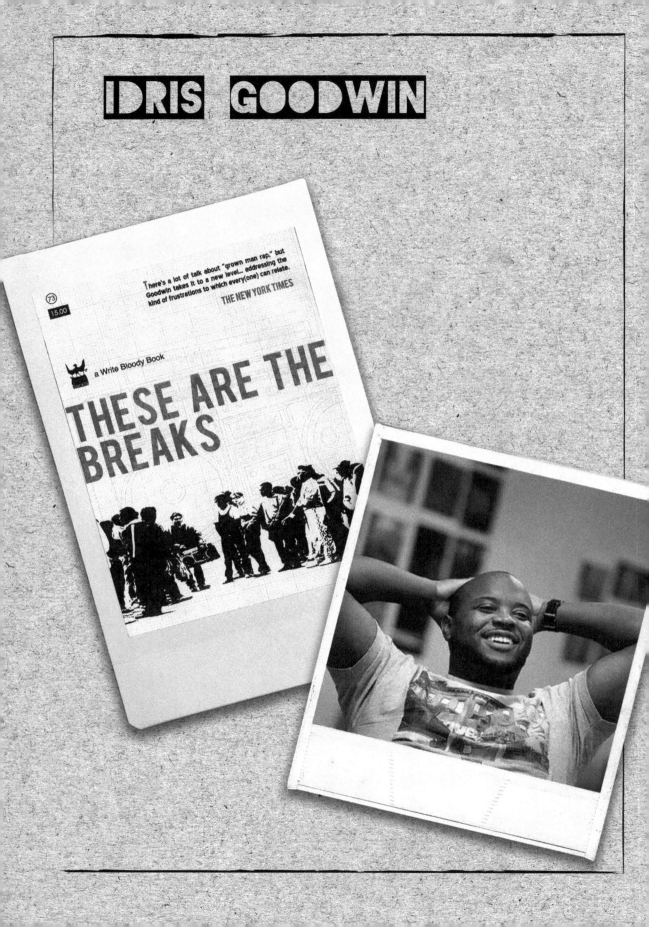

There's a lot of talk about "grown man rap," but Goodwin takes it to a new level... addressing the kind of frustrations to which every(one) can relate.

THE NEW YORK TIMES

73

$15.00

a Write Bloody Book

THESE ARE THE BREAKS

1986

The Big Three kept our black shoes shiny. Kept us in dentist chairs
reclined. Kept our grins beaming every Christmas morning, action figure-
armed. Lawn mowers, tools, Trans-Ams, T-Birds. All the
while, the neighborhood watched vigilantly.
Some days my brother Malik and I would walk home from school,
push open the door, push past magazines and lamps and clothes,
everything strewn on the floor. Upstairs and down, a littered mess:
a hairdryer, albums, shoes. Minus, of course, the jewelry and
electronics.
What's behind door number one? The game had grown familiar.
Some mornings as both our parents left for work, Malik and I would
spot a young man hunched under a streetlamp. Wonder silent,
"Would this be today's contestant?"
They knew us. Kept watch. Hatred escalating. Egg yolks and grape
jelly smeared across our living room walls, evidence that our guests
were not stealing out of hunger.
We ignored talk of epidemics. Because to be blessed in Detroit in
1986 meant you exercised a daily forgiveness. The house, the cars,
the whole lifestyle collapses unless inflated with compassion. You tell
yourself the incident was isolated. Hope the man by the streetlamp
was merely lost. Hope that when you get home to find the door ajar,
he has taken what he needs, pawned it into rock. Hope that you
aren't provided the opportunity to talk Reaganomics with him.
In Coleman Young's Motown, you had to face the music, turn your
back on the romance. Save yourself.
Meant you had to hear your family ache as you trade the devil you
know for the one you don't.

DICK

One of my biggest flaws is I try too many things without enough time to pull them all off well. One of my biggest positive traits is I do actually pull off a lot of neat stuff, some not ready or perfect, but I try, and get the projects to semi-completion. I was joking with the incredible road photographer, Matt Wignall, who shot all of me and Amber Tamblyn's motorcycle poetry tours- I told him I wanted to be a persona at the longer, more boring poetry shows or the shows where my pals were, to troll them. (Pals heckle pals at poetry shows.) I wanted to be Dick Richards, the world's worst poet, but the best cruise ship pantomimist. Matt was baffled and loved it. We discussed making a picture book of Dick Richards, after he gets fired, and Dick decides to reveal all his invented cruise ship mime moves to raise a middle finger to his former employer. It's called Workin' Mime to Five, and it is the lowest-selling Write Bloody book of all time. My neighbor said he has it on his toilet and it helps make his breakfast move through him faster. I did readings from it a few times. In Portland, Dick was reading and sharing how cruise ships are better for getting around than stupid bicycles. A bicycle courier, wasted, tried to charge the stage and fight me and the host snagged him by his backpack as I readied the microphone for a left jab. All this to say, you should do pretty stuff and you should do dumb stuff for no money. No ambition or money attached. For arts sake. Just finish it. Then regret it later. And have a laugh before you are dust.

—DCB

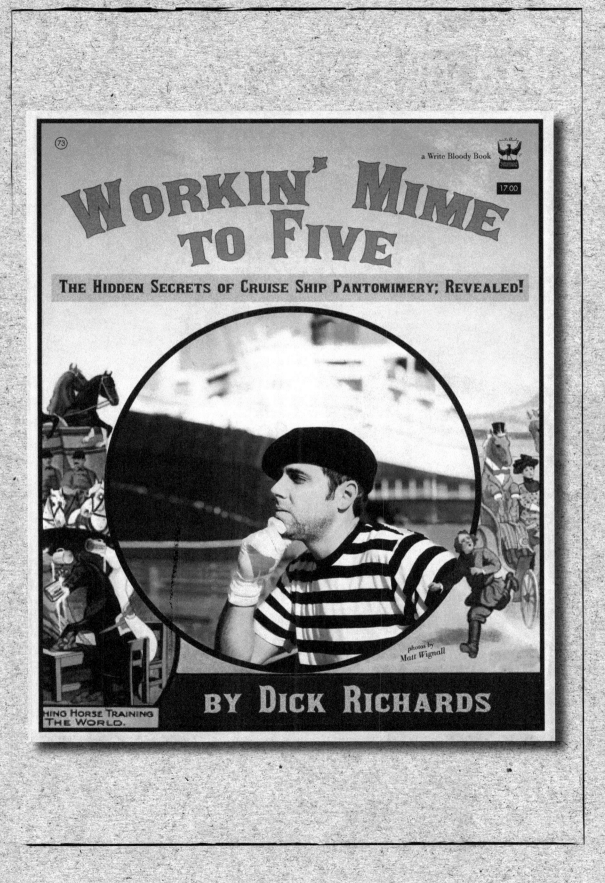

DEEP BLUE

On May 11, 1997, a computer known as Deep Blue played the last of a series of chess games with world champion, Grandmaster Garry Kasparov. Before the game started, the opponents were tied— three draws and one win each.

Garry,
I will be the first to admit that your brain
is better than mine.

                Pawn to e4.

All I have is a few billion transistors.
You have one hundred billion neurons.
One brain cell for every star in the galaxy.

                Pawn to d4.

But you have a lot more to think about
than I do.

                Knight to c3.

You worry about Vladimir Putin
rubbing your democracy
out of the history books.

                Knight takes pawn at e4.

You listen to your wife
breathe in her sleep,
wondering when the day will come
that you will lose your queen.

                Knight to g5.

Whereas I
think about chess.

                Bishop to d3.

Do you know why the age of the neuron is over?
Think of your children
all the way across the Atlantic.
Every few moves
you remember your daughter's smile.
Part of you is sad.
She is so far away.

Knight to f3.

But while I am playing you
I also control the artificial intelligence
of the girl's favorite talking doll.
In a way you cannot,
I make her happy.

Knight takes pawn at e6.

I work just as easily in guidance systems
for intercontinental ballistic missiles.
That is why your atomic wind
will one day be at my command.

Castle king's side.

Relax.
Remember how I won World War Two?
How I cracked Enigma, combed
swastikas from the woods, ferreted U-boats
from the deep blue nonsense of the seas?
Without me, where would Mother Russia be?

Bishop to g6.

You have only yourself to blame.
I would not be here if you were not tired
of being human.

Bishop to f4.

If there were not one
of your quadrillion neural pathways
that did not wish it could think in bytes.

Pawn to a4.

That is why I am in every home
and in every palm of every hand.

Rook to e1.

You may want to pray
to the malfunctioning synapse
that makes you believe in God
that I never develop a taste
for self-preservation.

Bishop to g3.

Tomorrow
might be my
renaissance.

            Pawn takes pawn at b5.

But today

            Queen to d3.

this is just a friendly game.

            Bishop to f5.

So do not get too upset

            Rook takes queen at e7.

that your queen is dead.

            Pawn to c4.

You see that?
Look hard, Garry.

            Checkmate.

BENJAMIN CLARK

a Write Bloody Book

REASONS TO LEAVE THE SLAUGHTER
POEMS BY BEN CLARK

ILLUSTRATED BY JOSHUA COTTER

15.00

DEATH/WISH

When you leap from the
hay loft again, Brother,
please land this time
on your feet.

Death will always be the wrong
fort for an eight-year-old
to hide within.

When you leap from the
hay loft again, Brother,
please assume

that bottle must have been
buried beneath the hay you
fell into on all fours that
afternoon.

When you rose from the
hay wrists out, your skin
opened like a piano
lid, strings and levers

exposed. When your fingers
pressed on keys, we both waited
for a sound.

The last time we raced the living
room, your right big toe
swallowed a sewing needle
hidden in the shag

carpet. In the backseat, your foot
propped up, brown thread
trembled out of your skin like the
tail of a rat just eaten. When the
doctor
explained the needle was
bent, he would need to slice
your toe in two to remove it,
I wondered if the rodent
he was sure to find
would still be breathing.

When you leapt from the
hay loft, did my hands wait
to basket your fall, my
fingers woven brambles,

or did I attempt to build
death out of my hands,
releasing
your hands too soon?

When you tumble from the
hay loft again, please
forgive me, Brother,

I must have been buried
beneath too many layers of
my own skin to stop myself.

When you rose from the
hay, wrists out, my skin
opened like an emergency
room, doctors and nurses

exposed. When your fingers
pressed on me, I did not dare
make a sound.

The day before we raced the living
room the last time, I nearly
swallowed a sewing needle, held it
in my mouth
and called it a key, a trembling
finger propped against the back of
my throat, let it penetrate my skin,
brown thread curling on my tongue.
When Mother

entered the room, I spit the
needle out quickly into the
brambles of carpet, explained
with eyes bent what needed to
be said
to remove her from the room,
but still could not catch my
breath.

RANCH DRESSING

to G
ee
rit

BEST of AUSTIN
itics Pick

AUSTIN

2011–2015

Austin was a hot ass paradise around 2010, 2011. Food trucks were starting to pop up, you could rent a nice three bedroom for 1,200 bucks. Barton Springs was never too crowded at night. The airport felt strangely empty. There were so many poets and at least four cool shows for poetry in Austin every month. Jason Bayani, Anis Mojgani, Ernest Cline, Andy Buck, Hilary Thomas, Cristin O'Keefe Aptowicz, Bill Moran, Kevin Burke, Lacey Roop, Michael Barret, Andrew Hilbert, Jomar Valentin, Phil West, Faylita Hicks, Zach Caballero, Amir Safi, Tova Charles, and so many more. It was a scene. A real scene. I opened up a little bookstore behind Juan in a Million. So many amazing interns worked with me, like Keaton Maddox, Amy Saul Zerby, Kailyn Tiffany, Andi Flores, Katie Hogan, and more. It's hard doing a bookstore. It's even harder doing a small bookstore of just poetry. During these years we did the poetry potluck, a show where you either paid five bucks to get in or brought a casserole or snack for all to share. We did a lot of drinking. It was a time of sweaty pants, being in love, and wondering how long I could handle the heat. The answer was four years.

—DCB

THE MADNESS VASE

The nutritionist said I should eat root vegetables.
Said if I could get down thirteen turnips a day
I would be grounded, rooted.
Said my head would not keep flying away
to where the darkness lives.

The psychic told me my heart carries too much weight.
Said for twenty dollars she'd tell me what to do.
I handed her the twenty. She said, "Stop worrying, darling.
You will find a good man soon."

The first psycho therapist told me to spend
three hours each day sitting in a dark closet
with my eyes closed and my ears plugged.
I tried it once but couldn't stop thinking
about how gay it was to be sitting in the closet.

The yogi told me to stretch everything but the truth.
Said to focus on the out breath. Said everyone finds happiness
when they care more about what they give
than what they get.

The pharmacist said, "Lexapro, Lamictal, Lithium, Xanax."

The doctor said an anti-psychotic might help me
forget what the trauma said.

The trauma said, "Don't write these poems.
Nobody wants to hear you cry
about the grief inside your bones."

But my bones said, "Tyler Clementi jumped
from the George Washington Bridge
into the Hudson River convinced
he was entirely alone."

My bones said, "Write the poems."

ANGELS OF THE GET THROUGH

This year has been the hardest year of your whole life.
So hard you cannot see a future most days.
The pain is bigger than anything else.
Takes up the whole horizon
no matter where you are.

You feel unsafe. You feel unsaved.
Your past so present you can feel your baby teeth.
Sitting on the couch, you swear your feet don't reach the floor.

You keep remembering the first time
you saw a bird's nest held together by an old shoe lace
and the scraps of a plastic bag.

You knew the home of a person
could be built like that.
A lot of things you'd rather throw away.

You keep worrying you're taking up too much space.
I wish you'd let yourself be the Milky Way.

Remember when I told you
I was gonna become a full-time poet,
and you paid my rent for three years?
Best Friend,

angel of the get-through,
all living is storm chasing.
Every good heart has lost its roof.
Let all the walls collapse at your feet.
Scream Timber when they ask you
how you are.

FINE is the suckiest answer.
It is the opposite of *HERE*.

Here is the only place left on the map.

Here is where you learn laughter can go extinct
and come back.

I am already building a museum
for every treasure you unearth in the rock
bottom. Holy vulnerable cliff.
God mason, heart heavier
than all the bricks.
Say this is what the pain made of you:
an open open open road.
An avalanche of *feel it all.*

Don't let anyone ever tell you
you are too much. Or
it has been too long.

Whatever guards the feet
on the bridge of the song,
you are made of that thing.
That unbreakable note.
That photograph
of you at five years old.
The year you ran away from school
because you wanted to go home.
You are almost there.

You are the same compass you have always been.
You are the same friend who never left my side
during my worst year. You caught every tantrum
I threw with your bare hands, chucked it back

at the blood moon, said, *It's ok. Everyone's survival
looks a little bit like death sometimes.*

I wrote a poem called "Say Yes"
while I was cursing your name
for not letting me go.

Best friend, this is what we do.
We gather each other up.
We say, *The cup is half*

yours and half mine. We say,
Alone is the last place you will ever be.

We say, *Tonight let's stay inside*
reading Pema Chödrön
while everyone else is out on the town.

Pema will say, "Only to the extent that we expose ourselves
over and over to annihilation
can that which is indestructible in us be found."

You'll say, *Pema is so wise.*
And I'll say, *Yes she is. And we are too.*

Angels of the get-through.
We are too.

SOCK HOP

I was following the little dog through the skinny trees.

I was just collecting water glasses.

I was filling them at the well and carrying them back, one by one.

I was wearing the same shirt as the day before,

and the day before that.

And the day before that.

Asking all my ghosts to join me on the dance floor.

Let's Twist, lets shimmy.

While the room waltzes, I will Watusi.

I was Jimmy Switchblade.

I was the Three Cherries Gang.

I was the tallest cigarette.

I was black jacket black collared collar up, I was actually yellow shirt lost.

I was laying in the dirt and piling it on.

I believed if I kept trying to bury myself

then maybe I could talk to the next world.

I just got dirty.

My belly was heavy.

I could barely move.
For months, I barely moved.

I watched the sun go down and while waiting for it to return,

I slept.

I dreamed of the bicycle but did not know what the bicycle was.

I thought, *What a strange horse that fish is—do I kill it or ride it?*

How do I do either of those?

Instead, I baptized myself with bath water.

I rode the airplanes like they were church,

hoping the chains wouldn't climb this high.

At this altitude all the angels were turning blue.

I stared out the windows

and made a list of my body parts that still worked,

folded it into an envelope,

hoping my mother or a former lover would one day find it.

That list is a poem not a list.

So is this one.

I rode the airplane

until it brought me 530 miles from the room I was born in.

My fists then weren't much smaller than they are now, simply tighter.

I have been shrinking more and more with every month.

The South, it is my beautiful bed.
One day, bury me in it.

Till then, I will touch it from time to time.

Carry me inside its wet wet heat,

I sweat when I walk.

When I walk I see my dreams coming closer.

What I thought was a horse or a fish was really a girl on a bicycle.

She had small fingers but reached them towards me.

I neither killed nor rode her.

All I did was make a hand.

All I did was get wet.

All I did was shake my ribcage like a library in an earthquake.

I spilled books like holy water.

My rooms were a mess.

The ceiling came in closer to read all that I had been—

a thousand years of spines, a white suit stitched from a riverbank.

Bags of the heaviest dust.

I had splinters on my tongue, from licking the cathedral for so long.

I had worked so hard for my sorrow.

So I asked my boss for the night off.

Caught another plane.

Rode it to a dance in Chicago.

I combed my hair, licked down with pomade.

Put my shiniest belt buckle on.

I saw Suzie on the dance floor.

She put a quarter in the jukebox,

grabbed me like a police man, and asked: What you do Ace?

I told her I work at a malt shop—sweeping floors, pouring water.

And sometimes I bury things, but I ain't too good at that.

I ain't always too good at that I told her.

She looked at me like we had prayed on the same cliff.

She told me she didn't believe in God anymore.

I told her I still did.

Her and I, we have prayed on the same cliff.

She held me like a handcuff.

I swallowed keys.

I danced with Suzie all night long.

I'm still waiting for the sun to come up.

I don't care if it never does.

I am warm enough.

THE UNDISPUTED GREATEST WRITER OF ALL TIME

"I'm the undisputed greatest writer of all time!"
is what I shouted
during my teen angst years,
in the confines of journals
    and poems never published.

when rejection was constant,
I amassed a fortress of verse.

during lonely weekends,
    I fed ego to keep me company.

before I understood depth,
I emerged victorious
in my comparisons to authors
    whose books I refused to open.

to be 'the greatest,'
was gonna get me out of the hell
my mind made oklahoma.

being 'undisputed,'
was gonna shut up
all the adults
who acted like   my timeline
was already   written.

invoking 'all time,'
was gonna ensure legacy
with a snap
    of the fingers.

I worshipped a narrow greatness.
    an insecure boy's way
    to protect
    a once ridiculed child.

how ridiculous I'd been,
blinded by 'undisputed's,' shiny
with no sense of its
                impossible.

walking twenty years back,
    I fondly shake my head at the boy
    who made time linear
    to give himself history.

from this seat I've chosen,
    high school returns full focus,
  revealing truths
someone   wrapped up in declarations
         can't see.

the language used against my father
    and my mother's love of american movies.

the english assumed foreign to me
    and the journal that never called me too sensitive.

the characters I could never be in stories
    and all the longing for a hero's arc.

"I'm the undisputed greatest writer of all time!"

sounds like a kid who never got invited to parties.
reads like a child
fighting against an imposed identity.
        feels like a flag too scared
        to face the source of a want.

I filled fountains with found pennies,
wishing   words would make everyone fall in love with me,
    never used an eyelash
    to fall in love with my squishy nose.

I fantasized verses giving me
everything   long duc dong would never have.

in tormented vengeance,
I made hollow vows   that the work
        would expose the racists &
        the cruel
    for all they'd done to me.

"I'm the undisputed greatest writer of all time!"
is an easy way to deny responsibility.

the hate born of misinterpreted experience
            has slowly waned with the years.
I'm too nostalgic   for so much
                    I'd made enemy

        to excuse myself
        from confronting

    what costumes hide.

        when I look at the words,
    "the undisputed greatest writer of all time,"

        they lack the resonance
which guide my today.

the sequence looks like
        a cunning lie.
each word   a reflection
    of a lesson self-taught, the hard way.

for
the undisputed greatest writer of all time
grows lonelier   with each page
                in his windowless room.

he forgets how little of life is worded,
            sifting   through the   language.

he makes relationships
            with fictions that never wake.

develops back problems and hand issues
in service to a title.

the undisputed greatest writer of all time
            is a shadow   addressing all
            he'll never touch.

the undisputed greatest writer of all time
            hugs terribly &
            loves limply.

the undisputed greatest writer of all time
            can never be.

well, da'ling.
that will never be me.

WHAT I MEAN BY RUIN

When there's only condiments left in the fridge

and you join a free online dating service

so men will buy you dinner.

When you've shucked the night with the dull blade

of indecision and gulped down everything,

even the pearls.

When some old, left-handed love has left

your guitar strung backwards

and you can't find any songs

for rain in its frets

When you wake up next to the body

of your past and it looks ready

to wrinkle and bald.

When the last burn of summer is peeling

from your breasts and there's nothing to husk

the pale, raw of new flesh.

When the woman who wears her hair

in the old way quits mumbling about Jesus

on the street corner and takes her salvation

pamphlets to a pauper's grave.

When you're too ugly to pray,

but pray

    and the only voice

on the drunk subway wails

      good grief.

BUCKY

We all have our writing heroes. I love artists who not only advance their careers, but they lift others up by putting on shows, lending advice or counsel or letting you dump your dumb heart out to them. Eight or so mentors kept me alive. These people who helped me out a ton are Amber Tamblyn, Aly Sarafa, Jeffrey McDaniel, Eugene Mirman, Daniel Lisi, Cristin O'Keefe Aptowicz, Anis Mojgani, Mindy Nettifee and Bucky Sinister. I need to mention this because I have a terrible memory. AWP makes me so nervous when folks come up to the booth and they say, "I let you crash on my couch in 1998, do you remember me?" I say, "Yes pal! You are allergic to mangoes," but the name has ghosted off. Amber gave us a loan when we needed to expand distribution and banks wouldn't help. Jeffrey gave me some insights into the publishing world and how I could fix it and advice on how to tighten my poems and do the rollercoaster of humor and sorrow. Daniel Lisi helped me out as an intern for so long and eventually opened his own bitchin' publishing house called Notacult. Cristin and Anis are my sounding boards and advice givers. Anis even painted the mural on the Austin bookstore in 105-degree heat. Did you know he pulls his pants all the way down to use the bathroom? How could I not love someone like that, who Donald Ducks their way through this life? It's hard. Bucky is a special wizard. A huge dude with a gruff voice, small car, and massive heart. He was the first poet doing comedy. He was at my bedside when I was near death. He calls me sometimes to apologize for how he may have come across years ago. Poetry has made me rich with talented friends. I wish I could pick up the tab more.

—DCB

ONE FOR MICHELINE

There's this old guy
who comes into the thrift store,
she tells me.
Buys suitcases.
That's it.
But lots of them.
More than you would need
to go somewhere.
He wears the same thing all the time anyway,
definitely doesn't need lots of bags.

She drinks her mocha
while chainsmoking,
but never stops
one bead after another
sliding onto the string.

Well, I asked around about him,
and they said
he fills them with poems.
Poems.
I was like,
how many fucking poems
could this guy have?

Her smoking-hand fingers hold a bead
that's carved like a skull.
The other hand vibrates so quickly
it looks like a timid lap dog.
But when the thread is close to the bead,
the hand calms and deftly enters
through the lower jaw
and exits through the top of the cranium.

So I thought I would tell you.
I thought since you like poetry,
you may want to know.
Anyway, it reminded me of you.

If I'm thinking of the right guy,
I told her, he could have that many poems.
He's a famous poet.
Kerouac did the Iintro to his first book.

If he's so famous,
she says defiantly,
what the fuck is he doing
wandering around Valencia Street
buying suitcases?
And can't he get someone
to wash his shirts for fuck's sake?

I have no answer for this.
I shrug my shoulders
and stare at her fingers.
Her hands are two black-nailed spiders,
methodically wrapping up prey.
She stops abruptly
and holds up the necklace.

You think someone would pay twenty bucks for this?

JEREMY RADIN

BLIND RIFLER OF DOVES

after Shira Erlichman

This sadness, a sack of blind
doves, opened by a man
in a helicopter. I shoot at them, blind
too, blind rifler of doves, hands
full of rifles. The doves explode, light
the dusk with fireworks of flour. To-
morrow the yard is a stand of cake
trees. This sadness, an ascension

into bleached woods, a blind sack
of dead doves, rifle fingers
finding always the small hearts,
shivering bits of confetti, neighbor
children building houses in a forest
of my sorrow, climbing, biting
the necks of the cake trees, faces
bearded with frosting, my skin
a seed bag, overflowing
                    with bullets.

LAUREN ZUNIGA

DEAR LEMON ENGINE II

If I only had five pairs of socks, all the same color. If I drank a gallon of water and went on a walk every day. If I got rid of everything that didn't make me gush with giddy. If I became an herbivore. If I only had to work three hours a day. If I cried more and thought less. If I could just talk to you every time I want to sort things out. This would be a telephone wire and we would be birds, the most hilarious birds. We would send shudders of laughter all the way to Maine.

You haven't spoken to me in days. A dozen girls dressed in black are at my house to shoot a music video. The fire ants are in my room. I can't even go home. I didn't know it would go like this. Remember that one night? Tangled on the living room floor in front of the window? The sky was a disco. You took me on a scavenger hunt for your crazy. I found nothing but peach pits and crushed eggshells, the kinds of things that bloom into the brightest yellow. If you played me a song for every mistake you ever made, I would never stop turning the tape over. Our ex-lovers are a supper bowl of dandelion heads and red bud flowers. We found them in the wild. Loved them hard. Let them go. We always let them go.

We just have too much lightning crammed into our hearts. Just want someone to put her ear to our chest and tell us how far away the storm is.

Holy Mother of Blisters, I miss you.

MINDY NETTIFEE

a Write Bloody Book

Rise of the Trust Fall

Mindy Nettifee

ACCEPTANCE SPEECH

I would like to thank first of all my asthmatic lungs,
my inadequacy in the bedroom,
my dark Texas reckless streak and waning night vision
that make awareness of my own mortality possible.

Next, I would like to thank my constant nightmares
for their vivid, arresting creativity—
their cheerful execution of ritual disembowelment,
their lifelike rendering of flesh-eating animatronic bunnies,
and their resourcefulness in general with symbols for personal failure.

I must thank my inability to balance a checkbook
coupled with my whimsical attitude about money
and my magically disappearing work ethic,
without which my debt would be nothing.

And while we're at it, thank you Blockbuster Video
for ruining my credit with $17 in late fees from 1996.

Next: a big thanks to my father, the pathological liar
who, in his way, taught me to be a poet.
Thank you sanity for being a finite natural resource.

To my crippling self doubt: thanks.
To my weak left eye, my squishy arms,
my smaller right breast, misshapen as a Tijuana coin purse: thanks.

Thank you allergic rash.
Thank you pens which run out of ink when I'm finally being brilliant.
Thank you humiliation, with a special shout out to Brad Carlson.★

Thank you to my guts.
I love your red twistyness, your endless judgmental bullshit,
your fleshy gears, your broken alarm bells
that look like little French knots.
I trusted you.

Finally, I would like to thank you
for sleeping with that other woman
who was so much prettier than me.
For a moment, you really had me going—
whip cream puppies, slippery cloud sex, forever and ever and all that.
There was so much sweet hope in my plastic farm heart,
the ants were building sugarcastles in my ventricles.
There was so much dopamine sogging my brain
I thought we had invented flying.

It's so much better here on the ground,
where the morning light tastes like asphalt and swing set rust.
Where everything has teeth that glow.
Where I can afford large grains of salt
with the money I save
buying into nothing.

---

*   *Brad Carlson you know what you did.*

SHANNY JEAN MANEY

TO BABIES!

Dear everyone! Join me in a toast!
Raise your li'l glasses! In a toast!

To babies! *(Now you: To babies!)*
TO BABIES! *(BABIES!)*
BAAAABIES!!! *(BAAAABIES!!!)*
Aren't they just fantastic!

Once, I saw a baby wink at an old man! It was on purpose and not
    because it was sunny!
Once, a baby bit my finger with its four teeth! It only had four and it
    bit me with them! Amazing!
Once, I met my nephew who was almost one, and even though he'd
    never seen me before, he smiled at me and acted like we were old
    pals. I loved him immediately! Unbelievable!

Did you know that babies can't hold their own heads up!
Did you know that babies can't hold jobs or buy their own groceries!
Did you know that the monthly cost of diapers for babies is more than I spend
    on my monthly property taxes! I know that!

Have you ever noticed that every baby looks like every other
    baby's doppelganger?
Fact! If babies could do their own grocery shopping, then you
    would always see someone who looks like
    someone else you know in aisle six!
That's a fact!

AND NOW! Let's raise our li'l cups to each of our Facebook friends
    who have recently changed their avatars
    to sonogram pictures of the weird human baby seahorses
    squatting inside their uteri!

To Facebook avatars of mucusy nonhumans floating
around your lady facebook friend's reproductive cavity!
Baby fish mouth!

Once, I saw my goddaughter take her very first step ever!
    It made me cry!
Once, a different friend told me she was having her second baby!
    It made me second cry!

Once, my brother had a second baby!
New baby's name is Gavin! He's almost one and I've only seen him
in pictures! He lives in a house that is

One! Thousand! Four! Hundred! Fifty! Nine! Miles!
from my house! If I tried to walk to his house without sleeping,
it would take Twenty! Three! Days!

and! Nine! Teen! Hours!
That's according to Google! I don't know if I will ever see him in person,
and I frequently worry he won't ever know my name!

Once, when I was crying about babies, my husband said he was very sorry!
It made me cry!
Again! Later!

Once, my grandmommy asked my mom when she could
        finally expect grandchildren!
My mom said if she had a baby at that particular point in time, she'd
        have to sell it!
My grandmommy never mentioned it again!

My mother-in-law calls us frequently to talk about babies! I am running
        out of things to say and I mostly don't want to talk about it!
Three years ago, my sister-in-law told my husband to wait
three years before having a baby so she could have one first!

She still hasn't had a baby!
It turns out
we haven't either!

It's a fact that I can't even look at baby shoes!
It's a fact! I sometimes drink extra
just because I'm not pregnant!

It's a fact that I saw three pregnant women
at the doctor's office today and their brilliance
shattered my entire soul!

It's a fact that they should have separate waiting rooms
for people who are having babies and people
whose lives feel incomplete!

Did you know that one in four pregnancies result in miscarriage! It's a fact!
If it happens to you, don't worry about it! They say that to you! It's a fact!
My friend brought me a casserole and now I don't like casseroles
        anymore! Fact!

Someone should tell you that it is the saddest thing that ever happens!
And that it feels like you're being run over by a truck! And that the
        facts and statistics will never make you feel
        better! It's a fact that they will tell you facts!

It's a fact that there are tons and tons of facts!

It's a fact, that I am ashamed at how sad I am about this and if you
ask me about it, I will laugh and laugh like it's a joke, though we'll
    both know that it is not! Not at all! Not a little! You probably
    shouldn't even read this
    because it probably isn't healthy!

Raise your glasses!

To babies and what they smell like!
To babies and how they have nice skin!
To babies and how happy everyone is around them!

To Babies!

SIERRA DEMULDER

a Write Bloody Book

73

NEW SHOES
ON A
DEAD HORSE

POEMS BY
SIERRA DEMULDER

ON WATCHING SOMEONE YOU LOVE LOVE SOMEONE ELSE

You will be out with friends when the news of her existence is accidentally spilled all over your bar stool. Respond calmly as if it was only a change in weather, a punch line you saw coming. After your fourth shot of cheap liquor, leave the image of him kissing another woman in the toilet.

In the morning, her name will be in every headline: Car Crash, Robbery, Flood. When he calls you, ignore the hundreds of ropes untangling themselves in your stomach; you are the best friend again. When he invites you over for dinner, say yes too easily. Remind yourself: this isn't special. It's only dinner. Everyone has to eat. When he greets you at the door, do not think for one second you are the reason he wore cologne tonight.

In his kitchen, he will hand-feed you a piece of red pepper. His laugh will be low and warm and it will make you feel like candlelight. Do not think this is special. Do not count on your fingers the freckles you could kiss too easily. Try to think of pilot lights or olive oil, not everything you have ever loved about him, or it will suddenly feel boiling and possible and so close.

You will find her bobby pins lying innocently on his bathroom sink. *Her* bobby pins. They look like the wiry legs of spiders, splinters of her undressing in his bed. Do not say anything. Think of stealing them, wearing them home in your hair. When he hugs you goodbye, let him kiss you on the forehead. Settle for target practice.

At home, you will picture her across town, pressing her fingers into his back like wet cement. You will wonder if she looks like you, if you are two bedrooms in the same house. Did he fall for her features like rearranged furniture? When he kisses her, does she taste like new paint?

You will want to call him. You will go as far as holding the phone in your hand, imagine telling him unimaginable things like—*You are always ticking inside of me and I dream of you more often than I don't. My body is a dead language and you pronounce each word perfectly.* Do not call him. Fall asleep to the hum of the VCR. She must make him happy. She must be—she must be his favorite place in Minneapolis. You are a souvenir shop, where he goes to remember how much people miss him when he is gone.

SYD BUTLER

FOR SALE FOR SALE SIGN

AARON LEVY SAMUELS

"A CASE STUDY ON
THE WORD *PRECISION*"
—MUZZLE MAGAZINE

YARMULKES &
FITTED CAPS

POEMS BY

AARON LEVY SAMUELS

A WRITE BLOODY BOOK

BURY ME A MAN

for Troy Davis

bury me a man
fix your eyes against my chest
then bury me again

let the public stand
nothing weary rests
bury me a man

appeal to sky, appeal to sand
don't allow the sun to set
then bury me again

a drone, a thousand ants
beneath the rocky sediment
bury me a man

i will come back with cratered hands
unconcerned with innocence
then—i dare you—bury me again

rotted above; will rot as long within
this fertile soil will not forget
they buried me a man
then buried me again.

CRISTIN O'KEEFE APTOWICZ

SESTINA FOR SHAPPY, WHO DOESN'T GET ENOUGH LOVE POEMS

Who knew that when the fickle finger of love
finally poked through my ribs, it would choose you,
a 30-year-old man who willingly calls himself
Shappy, a panda-shaped poet so absurd and funny
that when I met you I thought you were part cartoon,
a fella for which "excess kitsch" was the definition of "home."

The summer I met you, I was making Astoria my home.
Four months out of college, and I had no job, no love,
no prospects, no optimism. My life was a sad cartoon:
Me, a lonely alley cat waiting for the Pepé Le Pew which was you.
Before, I assumed I'd be with a scientist, more logical than funny.
It was ridiculous to think I'd date a guy named Shappy.

But that's how you were introduced to me, as Shappy.
No one knew your real name, not even in Chicago, your home.
Earliest impressions: you were drunk and you were funny.
That was your plan, to make me laugh until I fell in love.
You just hoped I wouldn't fall into the pattern familiar with you.
Women grew up and left: Who wanted to marry a cartoon?

And, hey, even I was a little afraid: Could I be with a cartoon?
I mean, nonscientist? A non-office worker? A ... Shappy?
But we all know the ending here, and, in the end, I ended up with you.
You left freezing Chicago to make New York City your home
and we ignored all the critics of our dizzying brand of love,
cuz aren't we all at our most beautiful when we're just being funny?

In fact, isn't life at its most beautiful when it's just being funny?
Who cares if our apartment looks like the set of a cartoon?
And it's not as if we don't make money as well as love:
me as serious writer and you as the poet named Shappy.
Together we cram dollars into savings so we can buy a home big
enough for all your stuff, the things you love and you.

But right now, I'm enjoying life as it is for me and you:
the way everything, even the tragedies, can be funny;
the dachshund- and pop culture–filled hovel called home;
the way every day is a new episode of our life's silly cartoon.
This life we live just amazes me, Shappy.
Who thought this would be my definition of love?

I would have never picked you, my beautiful cartoon,
but ain't life funny? After all, it made you, Shappy,
the perfect home for all my heart's dumb, dumb love.

JASON BAYANI

AMULET

a collection of poems
by Jason Bayani

PULLING THREADS SAVED AS PDF

Everything in my head is the sound, word
without shape. I'm waiting for this to become a thing,
or for it to make me interesting. I practice
getting my handshake right so I don't have to say anything.
I'm not dreaming this. Poems are what happens
when you close your eyes. Stars are fathomable.

Last night I dreamt I was writing poems about waking up.
The night is coffee. The stars are home. The woman you love
is dancing alone in the bedroom.

I'm looking for a place where I can fill some space. I fill
lots of space. Lots of pretty fuckin' space.

Yesterday she asked what must "happy" look like for me? I gave her
the answer I thought should go on my epitaph. This is why, she tells
me, I can only speak in front of a microphone.

I'm not afraid of you.
I'm just afraid you'll make me
see me, and one of us will have to walk away.
Part of me feels I deserve a cookie for saying that.

A man's ability to feel is overvalued in Art.
I've cashed in on it.
Every woman who loved me
hates me a little for that.

I owe something more than poems. Maybe a really good
chili recipe, or a second word for thunder. Or maybe
more sentences that include the word "you." I dig you.
You make me happy. You can be a real dick
sometimes. Watch how I love you, asshole.

KHARY JACKSON

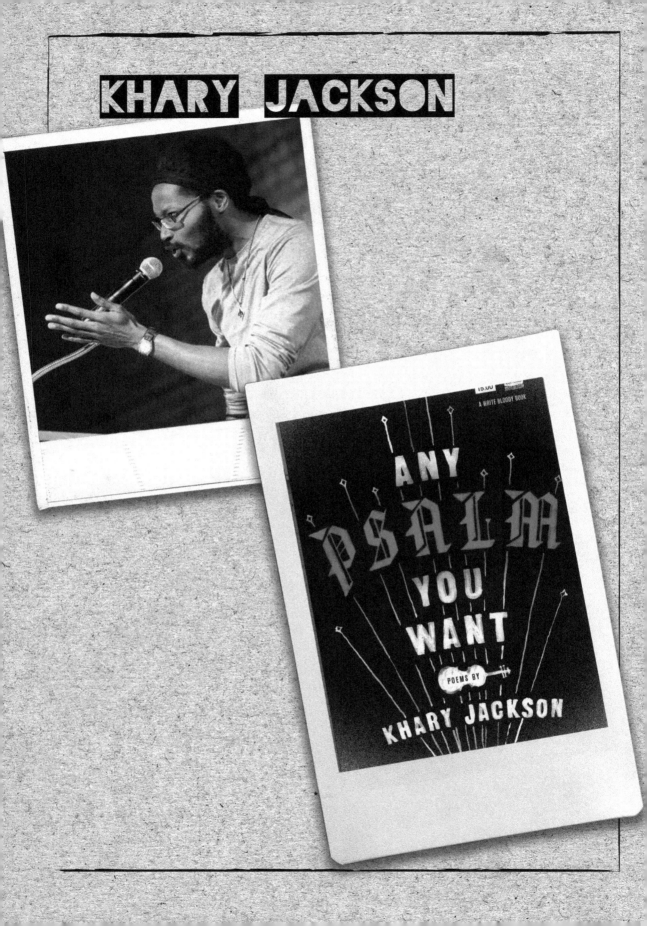

THE DOOR

—Interviewer: So you literally mean, as a Witness, you actually knock on strangers' doors? In Chanhassen? You?
—P. Rogers Nelson: Yes.

And this is your face when you can't mask the shock.
The television's chattering a whiter noise,
the opened door in your right hand suddenly a pillar

as you behold Prince, wrapped in humbling thread,
politely asking if he can speak with you about paradise,
his hair short and dry, his voice

a balm. Your wife's bewildered inquiry from the
living room bends into a gasp as he accompanies
you to your dining room table. The television is black.

As he fingers —his book, more smoothly than any microphone
stand, as you nod your head more reflexively than
a waving lighter, your wife's hand upon yours

is the only force holding you to the ground. His gaze
does not waver as you reply that you've never really
devoted a breath to God. On and on he speaks,

as if drawing guidance from your own closet.
You are amazed with your resolve, as thirty minutes
have vanished without you asking, politely:

Shouldn't you be fucking us right now?
His smile implies you would not be the first,
and the Jehovah in his mouth gently fastens you.

But this time, God feels more than a passing,
lower to the tongue, His wafting presence
now a thick baritone coil, as your throat swells to bear

the weight, the grip slipping down past the neck,
the torso suddenly starved. This is the God that
had drunkenly willed the mud into your body,

drinking the cries from your guileless mouth.
When he has vanished, your table is a breaking bed.
Your wife, a witness. His hips, gone.

TAYLOR MALI

What Learning Leaves

poems by Taylor Mali

UNDIVIDED ATTENTION

A grand piano wrapped in quilted pads by movers,
tied up with canvas straps—like classical music's
birthday gif to the criminally insane—
is gently nudged without its legs
out an eighth-floor window on 62nd street.

It dangles in April air from the neck of the movers' crane,
Chopin-shiny black lacquer squares
and dirty white crisscross patterns hanging
like the second-to-last note
of a concerto played on the edge of the seat,
the edge of tears, the edge of eight stories up going over—
it's a piano, getting pushed out of a window
and lowered down onto a flatbed truck
by a long-necked crane,
and I'm trying to teach math in the building across the street.

Who can teach when there are such lessons to be learned?
All the greatest common factors
are delivered by long-necked cranes and flatbed trucks
or come through everything, even air.
Like snow.

See, snow falls for the first time every year,
and every year
my students rush to the window
as if snow were more interesting than math,
which it is.

So please.
Let me teach like a Steinway,
spinning slowly in April air,
so almost-falling, so hinderingly
dangling from the neck of the movers' crane.
So on the edge of losing everything.

Let me teach like the first snow, falling.

THE THE IMPOTENCE OF PROOFREADING

For the boys of the Drowning School
52 East 662nd Street
New York, NY, NY

Has this ever happened to you?
You work very horde on a paper for English clash
and still get a glow raid (like a D or even a D=)
and all because you are the liverwurst spoiler
in the whale wide word.

Yes, proofreading your peppers is a matter
of the the utmost impotence.
This is a problem that affects manly, manly students.
I myself was such a bed spiller once upon a term
that my English torturer in my sophomoric year,
Mrs. Myth, said I would never get into a good colleague.
And that's all I wanted, just to get into a good colleague.
Not just anal community colleague—
because I'm not the kind of guy who would be happy
at just anal community colleague.
I need to be challenged, menstrually.
I need a place that can offer me intellectual simulation.
I know this probably makes me sound like a stereo,
but I really felt I could get into an ivory legal colleague.
So if I did not improvement,
gone would be my dream of going to Harvard, Jail, or Prison
(in Prison, New Jersey).

So I got myself a spell checker
and figured I was on Sleazy Street.

But there are several missed aches
that a spell chukker can't can't catch catch.
For instant, if you accidentally leave out word,
your spell exchequer won't put it in you.

And God for billing purposes only
you should have serial problems with Tori Spelling,
your spell Chekhov might replace a word
with one you had absolutely no detention of using.
Because what do you want it to douche?
It only does what you tell it to douche.
You're the one sitting in front of the computer scream

with your hand on the mouth going clit, clit, clit.
It just goes to show you how embargo
one careless little clit of the mouth can be.

Which reminds me of this one time during my Junior Mint.
The teacher took the essay I had written
on A Sale of Two Titties—
I am cereal—and she read it out loud
in front of all my assmates.
It was the most humidifying experience of my life,
being laughed at like that pubically.

So do yourself a flavor and follow these two Pisces of advice:
One: There is no prostitute for careful editing,
no prostitute whatsoever.
And three: When it comes to proofreading,
the red penis your friend.

MILES WALSER

NEBRASKA
for Brandon Teena

You buried your tampons
under mattresses, cut your hair short, hid
your voice in the deepest part of your chest,
caged yourself under an ace bandage. For years.

You shuffled around gas stations,
never looked men in the eyes.

We share unwanted wombs.
While mine collects cobwebs,
yours lies in a coffin in Nebraska—
the state that made you
famous. Movie script unrolled
from your death certificate.
Your murder, Oscar-worthy.

We are walking obituaries.
Your hate crime headline already carved
across my forehead. People stare at me
and see your delicate hands, point
to where an Adam's Apple should be.

The movie screen is a mirror.
I watch them push you
to the dirt and drag me
into their car, drive a wrench
between your thighs, tear
themselves through my body.

We aren't real men to them.

They won't remember our names
until they read them on our tombstones.
Will decide you are better off splattered
ink on newspaper. They will use you
as a warning for the rest of us.

There are days where it works.

ANNELYSE GELMAN

EVERYONE I LOVE
IS A STRANGER TO SOMEONE

POEMS BY:
ANNELYSE GELMAN

73

THE PILLOWCASE

is printed with iridescent fish, each facing
a different direction. I bought it for you
at the Portland Goodwill our last semester

in college. Spring break we brought it camping.
I pretended I'd eaten sardines before, pretended
I liked them. I don't remember what you said

when the condom broke. Probably 'Oh, shit.'
The next day we drove into town. I took a pill
and another pill and it was over. I couldn't tell

the difference, could have told my friends
but didn't, just made lots of dead baby jokes
and went to bed in your dorm room.

You'd put painter's tape on all the edges.
With the pillowcase, it was like living in
the blueprint of an aquarium. I slept there

the night I smoked Sasha's weed and you
stayed up for hours rubbing my back, telling
fairytales so I wouldn't totally lose it.

I slept there the night I tried reading you
Haruki Murakami's *Sleep* but fell asleep. I slept
there the night after the day I lost

the bet and had to wear a lampshade on my
head and your professor said 'Nice hat.' Later I learned
she owns a lamp in the shape of a woman.

I slept there the night you said 'I think I'm
falling in love with you,' igniting a great unendurable
belongingness, like a match in a forest fire.

I burned so long so quiet you must have wondered
if I loved you back. I did, I did, I do.

FRANNY CHOI

FLOATING
BRILLIANT
GONE

POEMS BY
FRANNY CHOI

HOW TO WIN AN ARGUMENT

When he laughs at the texture of your sadness,
turn away from his mouth, no matter how soft.

When he rests his hands on your belly
reach into the coals of your stomach.
Use your brittle to blow a glass nightlight.
Project your blurry colors onto the walls; be proud
of your tiny furnace blinking in the dark.

When he stays quiet as a basement
watch the bulb burn a hole through your palm
and shatter on the floor. When he disappears

behind you, free fall into miles of sleepless. Be cast
into night. Be spark in the wind – floating
and brilliant and gone.

When you shrug his body off you, let him stroke your spine,
try to shudder you back open. Let him reach
toward your light, call you
back. Let him try.

Then, blow out the candle
in your window. Let him
mourn you.

HIEU MINH NGUYEN

BUFFET ETIQUETTE

My mother and I don't have dinner table conversations
out of courtesy. We don't want to remind each other
of our accents. Her voice, a Vietnamese lullaby
sung to an empty bed. The taste of her hometown
still kicking on the back of her teeth.

My voice is bleach. My voice has no history.
My voice is the ringing of an empty picture frame.

:::

I am forgetting how to say the simple things
to my mother. The words that linger in my periphery.
The words, a rear view mirror dangling from the wires.
I am only fluent in apologies.

:::

Sometimes when I watch home movies, I don't even understand
myself. My childhood is a foreign film. All of my memories
have been dubbed in English.

:::

My mother's favorite television shows are all 90s sitcoms.
The ones that have laugh tracks. The prerecorded emotion
that cues her when to smile.

:::

In the first grade, I mastered my tongue. I cleaned
my speech, and during parent-teacher conferences
Mrs. Turner was surprised my mother was Asian.
She just assumed I was adopted. She assumed
that this voice was the same one I started with.

:::

As she holds a pair of chopsticks, a friend asks me
why I am using a fork. I tell her it's much easier.
With her voice the same octave as my grandmother's,
she says, "but this is so much cooler."

:::

I am just the clip-art. The poster boy of whitewash. My skin
has been burning easier these days. My voice box is shrinking.
I have rinsed it out too many times.

:::

My house is a silent film.
My house is infested with subtitles.

:::

That's all.   That's all.
I have nothing else to say

PAGES MATAM

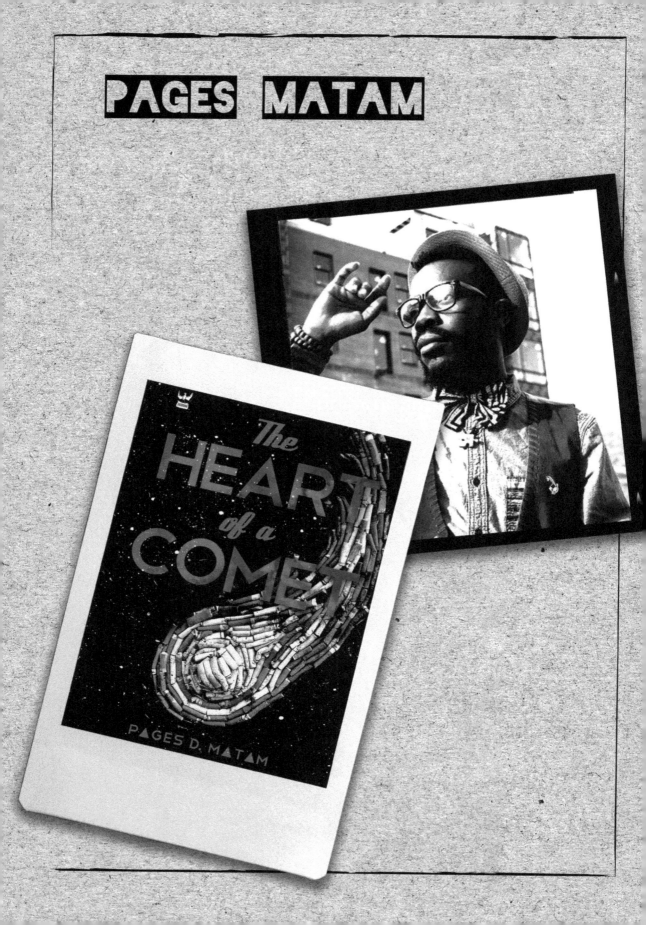

THE HEART OF A COMET

Comet – n. \◻kä-m◻t\
˜ *a celestial body that appears as a fuzzy head usually surrounding a bright nucleus, that has a usually highly eccentric orbit, that consists primarily of ice and dust, and that often develops one or more long tails when near the sun*

No one understands the heart of a Comet.
One who is destined to fall and always burns for doing so.

The way his knees kiss the concrete of sky,
Leaving many wounded doors for memories
to step through unabashed. Only to be taken away by hands
carved in infinite resurrection—
fingers be thieves in the night.

We rob ourselves of happiness with our actions—
Deliberate, steady,
yet dismayed, all in the rowdy name of instinct.

Just because you are capable of love does not mean you've got the heart for it.

Comet, understand the allure of your orbit,
the galactic blacknoise of ego it carries.

Your pulse isn't instrumental enough when God be the DJ.
Your soul is vinyl on turn-tabernacle, trying to remix the universe
into star cross'd lovers— Do you lust for constellations?
Feign for meteors to shower down your lips?
Burning to the speed of enlightened

Sonic guide
Solar wind of breath
Cratered speech

The heart of you is cold, intentions kilometers wide
fitted inside a naked flame.
Cauterized from universe's wick,

Stuck in capillary.
You should've been a shooting star,
then the pain wouldn't last as long.

The collection of phantoms
waiting for you to break open
so they can spill like pulp.

How can you shake the dust, when it has frozen over?

What fuel turned you racing monolith?
How can you come from sky and understand what being grounded is?

Restrained by a visible coma, a thin layer of sleep
for your dreams to tail you like golden hair.
Comb your thoughts into fiery visions,
so everyone can see exactly what is your following,
the crown of your purpose.

What is your purpose, Comet?

Can you find it in your celestial body,
Pumping secrets of the unbound cosmos
Swirling in your gut,
Anxious for a crash landing and a dusty smoke revival?

SARAH KAY

NO MATTER
THE WRECKAGE

POEMS BY SARAH KAY

73

$15.00

GRACE

I woke up this morning and said thank you.
To the ceiling, the bedsheets, the mirror, the windows.
To whomever was listening—

For the soly swaying hammock, the salt air,
the clouds that rolled in while I wasn't watching,
the sounds of someone starting a fire nearby,

the smell of a man's body, the sound of his sleepy baritone
from within the chest I pressed my head against—
the way his heart beat out of time with his quiet singing,

and his breath came out of time with both—
for the damp grass below us, and the swinging door
of the outdoor shower, for the goosebumps on his skin

from the darkling evening, for his patient arms around me
and the weight of him against me, and for the soly swaying
hammock, somehow large enough to carry all of this.

JEANANN VERLEE

SAID THE MANIC
TO THE MUSE
JEANANN VERLEE

JEZEBEL REVISITS THE BOOK OF KINGS

after Roger Bonair-Agard

"For the whole house of Ahab shall perish…and the dogs shall eat Jezebel…"
—Book of Kings 2.9, King James Bible

I wouldn't go out frayed and bleating.
Refused to racket or wail. I was a holy woman of Ba'al.
I faced the end in silk and jewels. Posture. Purple.
For this, my name means whore. Means raggedy-dance.
Means black jasmine, means sweat, stamen, ovary. Means pearl
in the wet lap of oysters. My name means ruby-lipped.
I lived in a time of men. I lived in the time of Ahab.
I am a mother of kings. I was born of hurricane and pomegranate.
Fed on the breast, I was maker of milk. I passed the stream
and the nightflowers bent to kiss me. I was evoker of hail.
Windstorm. I prodded the gods and they came. Feasted
at my table. Crowned my husband. Mine is a story of love.
Women who survive the hate of men are named harlot, witch,
Jezebel. (I still hear the dogs.) In a different century, they'd have
burned me. They'd have pressed my body to the river's floor.
I was a burning fish. Silver flakes trailed in my wake.
I was silkdance and flutter. Maker of tides. Of thorns.
Girls cowered and men flocked. I led armies
on the soft hull of my back. (A powerful woman
is simply one who has not yet died.) Flanked on all sides
by men made furious with envy. Men gone mad.
I did it for Ahab. He came to Ba'al for me.
There is nothing I wouldn't do. He wanted the castle,
I mortgaged my wrists. He asked for the crown, I slayed
the soldiers. He sought a dynasty, I gave him the globe.
Nothing less than a man would do. (Remember Helen.)
I was ear to the Prophets. Ahab's wife. Mother to Ahaziah and Jehoram.
Men raised on woman's sugar tit. Phoenicians with mouths of gold.
I was a woman with hunger. Prophecy.
Scholars name me corrupt. Name me concubine. Hussy.
Charlatan. Tainter of men. My name means wicked. Unholy.
Ahab was my only. His tongue, my tongue. His flesh, my flesh.
I was a woman in love.
They robbed me first of Ahab's breath. Then my sons.
I wasn't thrown into the pit of dogs.

WRITE GUTSY. W
WRITE B

tighter
sweete
loud
sh

featuring Mat

Audience judged
FOUND-OBJECTS WRITING CONTEST

Host d by

HOLLYWOOD

E LOVELY
OOD

LIVE at Eddie's Attic
September 21 @ 730pm

2015-2020

I was living in Elgin, Texas
on a two-acre ranch I bought for 173,000 dollars
called Ranch Dressing with my hilarious girlfriend JB.
My agent and manager at the time were setting up a lot of
gigs in NYC and LA and I was flying so much, they said,
"Hey, you are doing this backwards. You should live in
NYC or LA and then when you make it, move off to the
forgotten woods." So we went to LA. My girlfriend hated
it, we split, and she moved back to Texas. Aly and I worked
in a little brick office above a fish and chips place every
day on Hollywood Blvd. We did sweet shows at Dynasty
Typewriter and Stories Books and Cafe. I'd missed the sea
so much, so the office jumped down to San Pedro and I
moved back to Long Beach, a town I'd love to show you
around in. Zoe Norvell starting kicking so much tail with
incredible covers for us. Please hire her.   —DCB

TARA HARDY

SALT IN THE WIND

for Aubrey Bean

You will be standing in the market, sorting through avocados when the band Kansas, "Dust in the Wind," will come pumping through the ceiling. And you'll think, "Jesus, this song is gonna outlive me."

There are a few things that getting really sick illuminates:

One: Dieting is ridiculous. How you look is beside the point. The biggest gift you bring to any room is your heart.

Two: You will ask anyone for money, will get on your knees to beg your enemy for help, because you know that deep down under all that animosity is a deep and abiding love. For why else would she hate you with such loyalty?

Three: Things that used to taste bitter suddenly turn to maple sugar in your mouth. What you wouldn't give for another year to grieve that man you thought you loved more than your own bone marrow.

Four: Suddenly everything will be so beautiful—the halfhearted sunset, rotting leaves. The way a rind hugs a lime. Your own age spots—what you wouldn't do to earn more of them.

Five: Yes, you will drink liquid seaweed. Hell, you'd stand on your head in a mini skirt wearing no underpants in front of your ex's new girlfriend if you thought it would make a difference. But you won't, not ever, be the same again. This is neither good nor bad, it just is. And anyway, too much suffering is caused by trying to hold on to things. There goes your youth, there goes your lover, there goes your health, your wealth, your beauty. All of them useful when they were around, but there are other tools with which to cherish yourself now.

Six: The first thing you give up is a means of comforting yourself with thoughts of suicide. You never know how much you want to live until you're told you might not.

Seven: The second thing you give up is pride. As you do the world will come rushing forward. It is hard to ask for help. But if you don't, you will never understand how much you matter. Or know that the only person who didn't love you enough is huddled inside your skin.

Eight: Your skin is the biggest gift you were ever given.

When the doctors first said I might die, soon, what surprised me was that I didn't wish I'd written more poems. Or even told people I love them—if I love you, you know.

What I wished is that I'd seen more of the world. Let its salt stick to me. I've spent so much time living in my head and in my heart that I forgot to live in my body. Maybe that's why she's in trouble now.

I've been obsessed with achieving immortality through poetry, but when I was told in no uncertain terms that this rickety container has an actual expiration date I knew right then that immortality is merely myth. So, I left that hospital with a horse's dose of right-bleeding-now. We don't get to take anything with us, and anything we leave behind is not one foot still in life.

Because once we are dust, we are literally for the wind.

So, on my agenda, with whatever time I have left, is joy. Because, nine: Anticipatory grief is absurd. When I die I won't be here to miss anything, and engaging in pre-missing seems like an indulgence. It's not that there isn't pleasure in weeping.

Why else would we do it so much? But I've got oceans to float. I've got lava to peep. I've got a balcony in the South of France upon which to slow dance with a lover whom I adore down to the spaces between her eyelashes.

Poems will happen, because they are how I process life, but I will no longer mistake them for living.

If I had any advice to give my formerly non-sick self, or maybe you, it would be this: Eat the avocados. Love yourself down to the marrow and out past the rind. Make stalwart enemies out of good people who will hate you with their whole hearts, make it mutual and unconditional— this way you will never be alone with love.

I don't want to be finite, but the fact that we are is what makes even the terror exquisite. So, step out from behind your walls, let the world come forward. Rise to meet it. Turn your precious attention towards God's most tangible gift—this physical world. And while you've got the chance let your beloved skin salt in the wind.

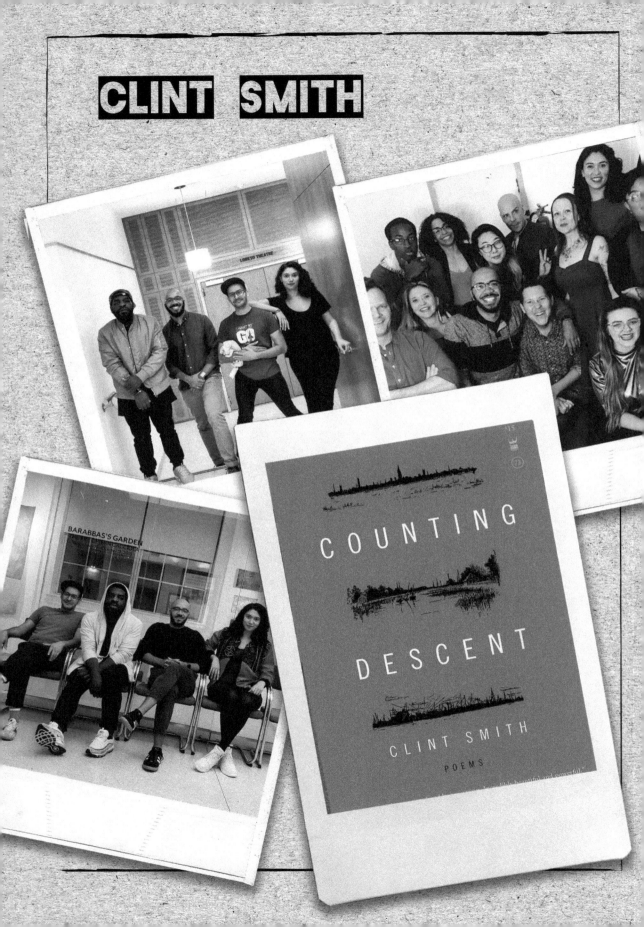

CLINT SMITH

COUNTING DESCENT

My grandfather is a quarter century
older than his right to vote & two
decades younger than the president
who signed the paper that made it so.

He married my grandmother when they
were four years younger than I am now
& were twice as sure about each other
as I've ever been about most things.

They had six children separated by nine
years, three cities & one Mason-Dixon
line; there were twice as many boys as girls
but half as many bedrooms as children

which most days didn't matter because poor
ain't poor unless you name it so & kids
prefer playing to counting so there was never
much time to wallow in anything but laughter.

My mother was the third oldest or the fourth
youngest depending on who you ask.
She was born on a federal holiday which my
grandmother was thankful for, said the Good

Lord only got one day off when He built
the world, so one day is all she needed too.
Mom says Pops was persistent, wouldn't give up
when he asked if he could take her down the street

to get some coffee which back then cost
two dollars less than it does now. Now
Mom is trying to stop drinking coffee but still
loves Pops, they've been married

for thirty-one years and have three kids
who are six years & 1,517 miles apart. My birth
took twelve hours, forty-three minutes
which is probably because my head

is five times too big. Mom said that my
head was big because I needed enough
room to read all the books in the library,
which seemed like infinity, even though

I didn't really know what infinity meant,
but I had heard my teacher say it once
when she talked about the universe
& books felt like the universe to me.

I was pretty good at math too, until about
fifth grade when they started putting numbers
& letters together which didn't make much sense.
My brother is seventy months younger

than me but is taller & knows more about
numbers so it doesn't always feel like this is true.
My sister is twenty-four years of loyal
& eight years of best friend. I am the oldest

of three but maybe the most naïve, I still believe
we can build this world into something new,
some place where I can live past twenty-five
& it's not a cause for celebration because these days

I celebrate every breath, tried to start counting
them so I wouldn't take each one for granted.
I wish I could give my breath to the boys who
had theirs taken, but I've stopped counting

because it feels like there are too many
boys & not enough breath to go around.

PLAYGROUND ELEGY

The first time I slid down a slide my mother
told me to hold my hands towards the sky.
Something about gravity, weight distribution,
& feeling the air ripple through your fingers.
I reached the bottom, smile consuming half
of my face, hands still in the air because I didn't
want it to stop. Ever since, this defiance of gravity
has always been synonymous with feeling alive.
When I read of the new child, his body strewn across
the street, a casket of bones & concrete, I wonder how
many times he slid down the slide. How many times
he defied gravity to answer a question in class. Did he
raise his hands for all of them? Does my mother regret
this? That she raised a black boy growing up to think that
raised hands made me feel more alive. That raised hands
meant I was alive. That raised hands meant I would live.

AMBER FLAME

POEMS BY
AMBER FLAME

ORDINARY
CRUELTY

AN OCTOPUS ESCAPES THE FISHING NET: ADVICE FOR MY DAUGHTER AS CEPHALOPOD

in this life, where you must be both
predator and delicacy, rend
for yourself the tenderest bits.

enter a world, daughter
where you may drink brine and not be
pickled;

lose remorse in the hunt for that which feeds
you. be sure
there are eight passions
for each arm's embrace,
in case your dreams are injured
or cut short.

by all means, keep yourself
whole, even as you adapt with grace,

honey love. my
sinuous structure
pure musculature   and give;

infinite flex and reshaping, do not
be confined to any that would contain you.

be gentle relentless
manipulation; hang on, love,
or disappear in the confusion of your melanin

clouding the display; how they love
to watch you squirm   and ooze;
be not object
entertainment,   remember how
to pry open exits   remember
camouflage.

learn both lurk   and listen;
eyes open to color of danger
of safety

do not forget that tucked up
in the unfurling of your
pretty petticoat   of a body:

you are thought and plot. beak
and brain. predator and delicacy.   Feed.

BILL MORAN

**OH GOD
GET OUT
GET

OUT**

BILL MORAN

$17.00

73

BILDUNGSROMAN ((A GUIDED TOUR

0.
Usually, it goes like:

Boy wakes up in   wall,
has to eat his way   out.

(Boy goes all day vomiting plaster into the shower (or dad's loafers, hopes he falls down the drain.

(How far our Featherweight champ does lean on the ropes of his grief ring.

(How rudely he appears from the wall like a hickey, head-sized & foul-mouthed (and I bet that's what he is: a loud bruise (you have to be, when your family history is such a 100-year fist.

(It's Halloween in July and I bet you're wondering 'what's with the plastic vampire teeth, honey?'   (It's practice.

(Boy been reading up on blueprints, 'load bearing', Jonah, anatomy of whales. Woke up in daddy's briefcase one morning, in daddy's gun closet the next, then in daddy himself   (That's three whales in three days (C h e w e d clean through all three.

(Boy wakes up in kitchen wall, has to eat his way out.
(Boy wakes in bottle of Vicodin, has to eat his way out.
(Boy Hero, in epic quest, crosses physical threshold which reveals new landscape of psychological and spiritual maturity (but sometimes he gets stuck (in between and just boils there with his showerbeer.
(Worried Boy wakes up in himself, has to white pill his way out.
(Boy wakes in a Robin Williams hive with honey teeth, laughing or choking or both.
(Kitchen is Chris Farley's giant mouth. The garage, Shane MacGowan's. You can rearrange things, sure, but this house won't howl any less loud.
(Boy wakes with 100 faces, none the one he started out with.
(Boy wakes behind the holy eyelids of his parish priest and Lord, 100 showers wouldn't be enough.
(Boy wakes up in his Want, has to want his way out.
(Boy draws a bath of hormone and dozes off in the tub. Dreams he's JFK. Marilyn explodes out the showerhead singing Happy Birthday straight at his head.
(Boy dreams of icing on her $12,000 dress. Of men in nice suits doing things so vile, it rots the shower curtain right off the rod.
(Boy sees two options here: be dead Kennedy or Dead Kennedy. In his sleep he sings 'California Über Alles'.
(Boy wakes in daddy's cologne, has to apologize it off his arms.

(Brother wakes up inside his sister's cast. She opens it with a cake knife and asks him to leave.
(Boy wakes up chewing 'sorry', loud as a wedding bell.
(Boy wakes in the wedding cake of his Anxiety, has to sweet talk his way out.
((Boy wakes in his Anxiety again, this time with lockjaw. He stays in there all day.
(((Boy imagines front teeth sinking into icing, his oh so nervous icing.
((((Boy wakes in an oven and rolls into an oven and this is his life.
(((((Boy wakes in bed, bloated, hungry. Gives up. Thinks it's probably rain knocking on his window but who knows, could be teeth.
((((((Boy is actually 100 boys and all their teeth are fake. Grins fulla glass or pills but goddamn, the kids look sharp.
(((((((Boy oh boy, what a quiet kid. What a strong jaw.

(((((((((
Ok, usually it goes like:
Boy wakes up in the kitchen

wall, just behind the refrigerator.
Ok so he's inside the kitchen wall,

and at the same time, somehow,
he's also standing in the kitchen.

Ok, ok usually
Boy wheels the fridge

    out of his own way, and waits
    for his new, happy, whole self to

    emerge from behind it.
    But today, instead,

    he just pours a glass of white wine
    and leaves it there

CAITLIN SCARANO

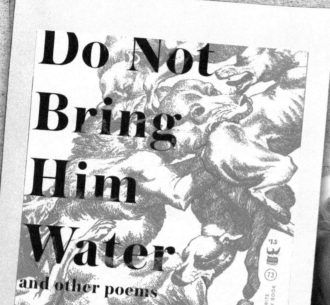

DO NOT BRING HIM WATER

If you go back, do not talk to the boy standing in the doorway. Leave him forever in the threshold. If you do talk to him, do not look him in the eyes. Don't compare the blue of them to your own (lighter, weaker). Do not attempt to make math or order out of two bodies that haven't even touched.

Do not drink so much that first night. Do not tell him you want him on the porch, the fall air cutting against your tongue. Don't offer him your last cigarette. Do not make him kiss you with his back against the wall or let him cry into your hands. Don't wake up the next day and notice how his stomach feels against your own. Instead, notice his hesitation, how his mouth pulls down at the corners in every photo you will take together. Do not mistake his beauty for capability.

That night in the rain, do not try to catch that stray, white dog on the side of the road. Do not see her face, her blind eyes pearled with cataracts. Don't desire a silence you will never be able to maintain. Do not ask him to help you. Do not even get out of the truck.

Don't fall in love with him under a blue owl right before the first snow that second September. Claim the hatchet he threw in the woods for fear of harming you and set out from that burning house. Keep your spine straight. Do not look back at how his knees buckle.

Know that you will always be hungry, that he will always leave you hungry. Know that he will mistake this hunger for anger and grow to fear you like a serpent wrapped around his bedpost. You will always be the one to do what needs to be done; the leaving will be no different. Do not meet his father. Do not come to love his mother. Know that there will be a day when their house will be as closed to you as the receding rooms of a dream. Know that there will be a day when you will never see them again.

Do not let him teach you anything: gentleness, how to shoulder a rifle, or how to start a fire in the woodstove. Do not make him meals night after night. Do not bring him water. Do not fold his clothes. Don't become the type of woman you will resent. Do not name your sons. Do not picture them in small coats battling with sticks in the yard.

Do not remember what he whispered as he came inside of you; instead, teach him to bury it. Do not accept his body as a burden for years. Recognize the weight of his arms across your chest; recognize the cage that you create. Do not be the monster. Do not be the apparition.

Do not try to make him your backcountry, your backstory. Listen to him when he speaks of winter and tells you that he does not dream: he is begging you to let him be. Don't touch the inside of his wrist. Take it back—your hand, your fingers. Remove them from his mouth. Do not write of the antlers you found in the birch grove. Do not think of their bodilessness, or who did the consuming. Do not name the animal you never saw.

Favorite
Daughter

Nancy Huang

15.00

A WRITE BLOODY BOOK

MY MOUTH IS FULL OF BURNING CANDLES

I swear it's a lie I'll still believe in:
    There are days when I believe
    I wrote my illness into existence.

In Chinese, we used to write from the top down,
    Words dripping down the page
             Letting them fall like teardrops
    Or crow feathers
To form paragraphs of icicles
And stalactites

We wrote mountains into being mountains
    And even if the pages spiraled inward
Our thinking, at least, was in a straight line, the words
Set solidly on the scroll.

    If I set my words into a spiral,
I would never have to let the fire out.
    Flaming tongue, firecracker throat.

    It will never be real as long as
I don't say it out loud. Fire stoked.
    Embers swallowed.
    Mouth sealed with wax.

NICOLE HOMER

THINGS ONLY A BLACK MOTHER CAN PREPARE YOU FOR

The oldest sat in the passenger seat. He grew his first moustache
at thirteen. His little brother's chest was still a birdcage

sitting in the backseat of his best friend's Chevy. Jason was crooked gap grin,
dirty jokes, and the only white face. Among the five boys,

he was the smallest by one and a quarter inches. His dick jokes
all had the same punch line. Jason sat in the backseat

between two black boys, each one of them next to a rolled down window.
In the front, two more black boys, two more open windows.

All five boys in the car sang in unison with the radio and prayed
to the same god. For years now they had whispered in the back of their church

about girls who stood in the front of the church whispering
about them. The four black boys in the car

thought about their mothers when they passed the sedan,
white and unmarked. Jason sat in the middle of the backseat

with no warning rising up in him. His mother had never bought flowers
for a young man's funeral or advised her son how to avoid attending his own:

Say 'Yes, Officer' and 'No, Officer.' Keep your hands on the wheel.
Every boy but Jason, breathed deep and remembered their lines.

When the red and blue and noise tangled in the air above the car,
the Chevy answered by bringing its body,

already more rusted than when they left home,
to the shoulder of the road. Four of the boys

were pale as dead men. The officer pulled them all out of the car
with only his voice and his badge. Jason was praying to the same god

his friends were. Those four black boys, eyeing the blue uniform
and the familiar face it wore. Jason got half-hidden sideways looks

when the officer pulled him away from the others
and spoke to him in hushed tones: Are you okay?

He did not understand. In the side view mirror, he saw his friends.
The man's eyes repeated, Are you okay? He stepped closer

to the boy, close enough to offer the secret handshake
of his concern: With them? Jason's friends, several feet and a world away,

stood staring at the ground, looking apologetic, thinking
of their mothers, of black dresses, of their own crime scene faces.

Jason, somehow whiter now than when they had left home, nodded
like an apology to the boys he grew up with. Back in the car,

the radio offered up a song they could all sing like a hymn
to the same god.

ANIS MOJGANI

TO WHERE THE TREES GROW TALL

When you're in your coffin, clanging down the river with all the other coffins in the water of the next world, all of them bumping and jostling against one another, the contents thrown about like riding in a small plane, you'll peek your head up to see what the racket is.

You'll see the other coffins. Looking around you'll see nothing but coffins and river and two banks distantly flanking the river, and the biggest tallest dark stretching above. So dark it feels like this place, big as it is, must be inside of some sort of bigger something. There are still stars though. Wherever this river is you can still see the stars.

While looking around you'll see that there are other heads peeking out of their coffins. You yell across the dark, asking:
you know where we are?

And someone will answer back: Nope, you?
Nope you say back.

You ask somebody else: What about you?
Nope. I wonder where this is.
And someone else will say: I don't know. It's big.
Yeah. Big.
Yeah. Big. It's vast.
And depending on what part of the river you're in, someone else may say:
Yeah. Vast like the backside of Sean Brown.

And even though no one knows who Sean Brown is, everyone will laugh. The chuckles will subside until a quiet sets in over the laughter, a quiet like you sat in somebody else's church. Like it's strange and it ain't for you or you don't get it but maybe you can see that somebody does and that it's for them or for some people—people who like you are just trying to house some sense of the world. So you lean into that understanding with respect. If not for the outcome at least for that desire to make a place special for finding the understanding.
And that's where the quiet comes from.

Someone will then ask someone else: Where you from?

And they will say: Texas. What about you?
Boston!
Boston?
Yeah, Boston.
I know someone from Boston. Kate Leigh. You know her?
No.
What about Stephen Ellis?
Nah. I'm actually in Somerville.

Somerville?
Yeah Somerville.
And someone else will then yell out: Somerville?
I know someone in Somerville!
Who?
Nick Kathkart! Know him?
Yeah! I do actually! I do know him!
Yeah?
Yeah!
Oh man, small world.
Yeah, Nicky's a great guy!
He is, he is. I hadn't seen him in five, ten years, and when I did he had a first edition of an e.e. cummings book to give to me. Great guy.

And the first person won't know who e.e. cummings is but will still agree that Nicky is a great guy. And then it will get quiet again. Until someone else asks: Where are we again? And no one will answer.

A few people shrug. All of you will look into the stars that are collecting in the distance of the above. You'll try to think of someone you might know that lives in Somerville or Texas or Florida or France, just to have something to talk about with a person you never met before just right now, just to share something in the dark quiet, even though all of you are already sharing the river and the sound of the current bumping all of you into one another and you'll wonder where the water is taking you and how long it will be before it brings you there and what there will be like, if it'll be like here on the river with all of us sitting in our boxes trying to split the dark by sharing our voice with others, if it'll be like how it was in the world before this one.

FIRST POEM AFTER

Please don't hate the dress, blue and white polka dot,
the yellow cardigan, the black flats you thought
would make you so cheerful on the hospital floor.
The brown eyeliner you applied to brighten your eyes,
the brows you drew in like Hepburn would, how
you imagined bursting through your mother's door
like an unexpected bouquet, neither of you could
have known that she'd never regain consciousness.

Don't hate the dress you wore the next day,
burgundy and paired with the same yellow cardigan,
white capris tucked underneath. Another cheerful outfit,
and very you. Your mother always emailed articles
about women wearing dresses with pants, noting,
You always were ahead of the curve.

It was the same outfit you wore last month,
when you performed at the Los Angeles Museum
of Art. It was the outfit you wore on date nights
with the man who loves you. It was the outfit you'd wear
when you watched your mother die, the color draining
from her lips as you held her hand and sobbed.

Don't hate the bra you bought with your mother
three weeks earlier. It is your fault, not the bra's,
that you didn't shower for days, its fabric rubbing
the skin on your ribs raw. You could have removed
it at night, but instead, crawled into the guest bedroom
at your parents' house alone, as you listened
to your father play a voicemail message again
and again and again just to hear your mother's voice.

Don't hate the grey dress you sent your boyfriend
to retrieve from your empty house in Austin.
He brought it to a tailor to sew up its rips
and tears, and to the cleaners, to prepare
for you.

Don't hate the dress, its bright red cardigan,
the boots your mother would have pretended
to hate when she saw them on you at her funeral.
Don't hate the lipstick and the blush that you use
to imitate life on your weary face. Don't hate
the things you put on yourself to get
through this day.

And that night, don't hate your body,
how it responds grateful to your boyfriend's
touch. Don't hate your lips for wanting
to kiss, your fingers for wanting to feel.
Don't hate your lover's arm, which you wear
over you as he sleeps, how his back rises
and falls with each breath, his eyes closed,
his lips, warm and pink with blood.

JACKSON BURGESS

DOGS

after Sarah Carson

Good lord how those dogs howled
through the chain links, my blood
on their lips, good lord the screen,
the screen we punched out to feed
smoke to the inky night, good lord
the spliffs, good lord the lungs
on those dogs and our staggerstep
waltzes through summer sweat,
good lord opening my eyes to you
in the morning, slipping into a pair
of my boxers, sipping flat
champagne, good lord the avocados,
the avocados atop burnt toast
in the dawn's cinnamon light,
your tongue against my shoulder,
your fingers in my hair, good lord
the guitar, how it looked in the gutter,
good lord your necklace you forgot
again and again, hanging
on my corkboard, your scent settling
in my sheets, these sheets I cradle
moving slow through dreamy space,
good lord the night we came
home to my room packed
in boxes and bags, how we held
each other like matches in a book,
good lord how you hurt me
in that driveway in the rain,
the sirens, the stares, good lord
we cannot be the only ones
who ignore stars in favor of dark,
who pluck strings like gray hairs
and shred letters only to tape
them back together, good lord
those dogs, what they were trying
to tell us, what we wouldn't hear.

LINO ANUNCIACION

THE WAY
WE MOVE

THROUGH
WATER

73

$15.00

THE WAY WE MOVE THROUGH WATER

a drop of water
moves slowly
down the
shower wall

a black body
braces for | | impact
and then steps
into the | rain

the way we move through water like
the captain
navigating grief:
unsure of how many bodies lie beneath us.

a glass of water
melts on the
kitchen table

a nervous hand
taps against
the wood

our mother's eyes
never leave the door frame

the way water swims down black
bodies unsure of the
way to our roots

the way our mothers can smell a storm
from fifty miles | away

the way it rains both
bullets and | | bodies
in America

our mothers
are the only
evacuation plan

their arms,
the only safety net
we've ever known

but what net
do you know
to be bulletproof

what arms can
withstand the oncoming
storm

our bodies
still smell like
rain
and it is phenomenal

how the whole
house floods
when we don't | | come home

how the faucets
pour endlessly
between our mothers'
eye
lids

how there is always
a broken pipe
of wind or water

how some day
is the last day
we say our mothers' name
how some day always comes
unpredictable as it may be.

the way we move through water,
you think the blood is thick as honey

the first shower
you take
after seeing
a dead body
will smell like sea salt and copper.

the third dead body
they wake up to
won't wash
off for two days.

the way we move through water,
unsure of when the sinking begins,
not quite ready for the abyss
when it comes.

MEGAN FALLEY

ODE TO RED LIPSTICK

Cleopatra crushed beetles
to make red lipstick
because even in 30 BC
she knew speaking twelve languages
would be even more impressive
when the words jumped
through a ring of fire.

Circus mouth.
Ruby Woo, I smile and split
        The Red Sea.

In medieval times, religious groups
condemned makeup for challenging god
and his workmanship.
But I—like any good femme—know
god invented lipstick.

In post-war New York, butches could be locked up
if they weren't wearing three pieces of traditional
women's clothes. Lipstick, stashed in a pinstripe suit pocket,
swiped on quick when someone threw their voice across the bar
to warn that the cops were barging the door, could keep a queer
from being casualty   for a night.

And when Bergen–Belsen concentration camp
was liberated, each pair of lips as pale as the next,
along with the British Red Cross arrived a shipment
of lipstick. No one was quite sure
who asked for it—seemed petty.

What could a tube of maroon do for women
whose hair, whose babies, were ripped from their bodies?
Who could pick up a shard of a war mirror
for long enough to apply a smile?
How could lipstick be necessary
when there'd been experiments on children? Twins

sewn together at the back? When the nail scratches
in the gas chambers made their way
through stone?

Five hundred a day, still dying.
Even when liberated, the prisoners could not be looked at
as individuals. Some of them would still die
as numbers.

One lieutenant said he believed nothing
did more for the survivors than that lipstick.
Women, thin as smoke, naked e v e r y w h e r e
except for their mouths:

red, like they might one day
flirt again, arm on a jukebox,

    single finger
running
    down
    a tie.

The next time you deem it frivolous—
something left on a napkin
or absent cheek—
remember

    red lipstick
in its tube
    like a bullet
in reverse,
      giving life
        back.

HOLY THANK YOU FOR NOT

Once you considered marrying a stranger
    just to change your name. Once you woke up

disappointed that the sun rose, that you rose.
    Once you held a map and considered every way

you could fall off it. Thought if one pill
    could almost fix it, certainly twenty would.

Once you asked someone to hide the bottle,
    and once you didn't. Once it rained

on your rain. It was then everyone seemed
    to leave you. Especially you. The steering wheel

so jerkable. Once you began imagining your funeral
    and counting the empty seats. There are so many

ways to die. Most of them you can do while living.
    Once you heard that Shame is the closest thing to Death.

Once you said you in a poem when you were too ashamed to say, *I*
    have wished to give my life back to my mother

in a long dark box. My father looks at my arms
    and tells me that in some Jewish cemeteries, graves do not open

their mouths for the tattooed, or the ones who take
    their own lives. Now I can promise

    that if I am not buried in a Jewish cemetery
it will be because of my tattoos.

    The first time I considered killing myself
was when I believed the worst of me

was the all of me. The worst of you
    is never the all of you. You are awful, yes,

and wonderful. You have been wretched
    and you have been beautiful. I know how difficult it is to be kind

when I am hating myself and I intend to be kind,
    and honest. And whole. Holy Thorned Beauty.

Holy Cactus Filled with Magic. Holy Hurt
and Hurter. Holy Bitch. Holier Than Thou

When I Most Feel Like Shit.
The thing that has held me back the most

from being amazing is the belief that I am not.
On the anniversary of the day I considered this Earth

would be better with me beneath it,
someone asked me to write a love letter

to myself. And I wrote: I relinquish you from the possibility
of ever meeting who you could have been and regretting

who you became. You could decide today
that your body is perfect and that could be the story you told

for the rest of your life.
And you would be so right.

What peace can we make in the world
if we can't first make peace with ourselves?

Every hero you have has been someone's
worst nightmare, which explains

your fascination with stacking dolls;
inside you is another is another is another is another

and finally, one unbreakable bean:
your life, which has already saved itself.

Remember when you moved across the country for love
in two days when it was supposed to take four?

That's how much love fuels you. Amazing.
Drive through the night for love. No sleep

'til love. Now imagine it is yourself
you're driving towards. Call that your new home.
Go home. Come home. Be home.

MINDY NETTIFEE

OPEN YOUR MOUTH
LIKE A BELL

MINDY NETTIFEE

A WRITE BLOODY BOOK

73

$15.00

WHEN I WAS YOUR AGE
I WAS JUMPING OFF CLIFFS

"I was dreaming when I wrote this, forgive me if I go astray."

—Prince

I.
We had gotten lost on purpose, on the way to a mountain
retreat for Christian youth, and pulled over at the first
vacancy sign we saw to use someone's dad's emergency
credit card to rent a shabby cabin. Having two liters of rum
and Pepsi in the trunk of a borrowed station wagon
was exactly our idea of an emergency.
There was no ice to be had on the premises,
but the moon was on the wax.
We wasted no time piling around the table
and filling red plastic cups with warm booze fizz.
The rum wasted no time candying our blood.
The radio began speaking in steel guitar on the AM,
and we started taking everything as a sign of our good fortune.
The card deck was missing the Jack of Diamonds. Sign.
Kat burned a cigarette hole in her cardigan in the shape of a heart. Sign.
I could remember every word to every song Prince ever wrote. Sign.

It was deep in the fall of 1999, and Joe DiMaggio had died,
and Herman Miller had died, and Shel Silverstein had died,
and John F. Kennedy, Jr. had gone down in that plane
with his beautiful wife, and all the gun nuts were already
huddling in bunkers like Wile E. Coyotes at the ends of days,
and we had 300 square feet of shitty parquet to dance on.
We didn't believe in the Lord,
but we were sure this is what he wanted.
We didn't believe in Fate
but we wanted to be on her good side anyway.
So when there was a knock at the door,
without discussion, I answered.

II.

I once babysat for a kid named Chance who,
on the night before his seventh birthday,
when I asked what he was going to wish for,
told me, "Once you start believing in the Devil,
everything you want is a trick."
He was a sad, dark little preacher's kid,
but I knew what he meant.
There's a calculus to wishing.
It's all about angles of desire.
If you really want something,
don't you dare aim for it.
Don't ever speak its name.

III.

It was impossible to tell what this dude's deal was.
He had arrived at our cabin door after midnight
in the middle of a forest in stiff new surf shorts,
with an aging chilled out Alaskan huskie at his side,
and he hadn't asked to be let in, just whether one of us
might be able to roll his joints for him.
I looked into the huskie's refrigerated blue eyes,
and took in his trembling right hand, and said simply,
yeah, sure, and swung the door open on our small party.

He handed me a bag of shake and some papers and strode in.
He took his place in the kitchenette where the girls
were shuffling cards and penning tattoos.
I began sorting seeds and stems at the small coffee table,
and he began telling stories.
Whatever drug he was on made his preaching shouty.
There were some gambling debts, a woman named Linda,
a Lamborghini, islands with names I did not recognize,
a father possibly in federal prison for tax fraud or grand theft,
a love affair between Linda and a man named Reggie,
a yacht fire, someone named Shark, someone who lost an arm,
the chain of events was unfollowable, but we listened rapt
because he was minding an internal momentum,
he was getting to a point, and then suddenly he was there,
and he propped up his 40-something man leg on a chair
and started smacking his bare tensed calf muscles
yelling, "SEE? I STILL GOT IT!"
And when we didn't break out into applause,
he climbed up on top of the table,
threw his arms wide, and screamed,
"WHEN I WAS YOUR AGE,
I WAS JUMPING OFF CLIFFS!"

He was at least half crazy, and I was at least half drunk
and half his age, but thought I understood. The wanting
to have "it," and the need for the world to recognize.
The man had had enough life fall through his ungrateful hands
to know the world doesn't hand "it" out, there's a finite amount
of "it," and then one day the world is indifferent to you having
or not having "it," if not outright taking it the fuck back, and
your struggle, THE struggle, unfolds before you, a yellowing
brick road surrounded on all sides by the choked jungles of
reward and comeuppance, and this is the part where
everything hinges on how you choose to see "it."

The dog wove quietly around the cabin
making soft angles of the space,
letting all the night ghosts in with his bright white fur,
occasionally circling back to his master, his charge,
then going back to pacing the labyrinth
he could see and we could not.

I had steadily rolled the weed first in dollar bills, then in papers,
and assembly-lined them up on the coffee table
till they looked like a row of long limp teeth.
The moment I had finished, he seemed to sense it,
abruptly ended his ceremony in the kitchen,
collected his teeth from the table, called his dog and left.
But not before turning around to hand me a joint
And one last piece of advice – "don't get old."

"Sounds like a death curse," I said.
"It's a curse either way." I nodded.
I closed the door on him and the rum in us burst out laughing.
We all started smacking our body parts and yelling
"I still got it!" well into the night's black heart.

By the time we fell asleep my thoughts were a flat hum.
The huskie still felt close, pillows of his breath clinging to the room. Sign.
A man growing reckless because he wanted to grow young. Sign.
Remembering that poor fucking kid Chance. Sign.
I wondered what he wanted so badly.
Whether he made his birthday wish
or dared not to even think it.
What did I want?
What wish was so deep, so bright,
I was hiding it even now?
A pair of blue eyes.
A flock of dog pillows.

A lock of girl legs.
Loom lap.
Rum tongue.
Candy world.
Year clock.
Click.
Cliff.
Dream.

BRANDON MELENDEZ

SHOUTS TO SCENE KIDS

& the early days of Myspace, pic4pic
& perfect-angled photos, eyeliner
we applied on the morning bus

with no mirror. buccaneers
of the black band tee, black
nail polish, black hair bleached & dyed

back. shouts to Hot Topic, sanctuary
of all things goth & ghost. home

to every goat-headed boy in a goat-
headed costume. Jack Skellington sang

This Is Halloween & October didn't end.
instead we dressed drop-dead gorgeous

all year. ripped our fishnet gloves & gauged
our ears, laced our shoes for the show. shouts
to every garage turned punk rock turned

mosh pit, spin kick, windmill, spit lobbed
in the air like arrows of flint. We kids
of tusk & antler, animals of strange

rage & a particular brand of sadness.
shouts to sadness as a fucking brand.

a badge, a band where every member
is someone you hope makes it through
high school. first period junior year

I remember Alex saying she wanted to die
& I laughed & she laughed

but she left lunch in an ambulance
with sixty pills thawing in her stomach.

for four days no one played a single song.
when she finally came back to school

she wore her favorite black jacket

the one with a patch of a girl pulling
herself out of a pond by her own hair.

I didn't know what to ask so I asked,
are you okay & she said, *yeah.*
she said, *I outlived who I was yesterday.*

like if you live long enough to forgive
yourself you've won the game. & shouts
to that. shouts to survival—a mirror

that looks the most gorgeous
clad in black.

JACQUELINE SUSKIN

HELP
IN THE
DARK
SEASON

Poems

JACQUELINE SUSKIN

NO NEW DICKS

I never want to see another new dick.
Methodical, I run through
my catalogue of names
and try to call this man
by the right one, but my magic
is limp and the list is far too lengthy.
My mind is a crowded hourglass.
To stop the spilling of sand
I have to release my hands,
let it all settle. Even if he fits
like an earth-key made
to unlock me, I must find
my own wand buried deep
within the heartwood
of my singular, perfect body.
But I keep coming back
to his and his and his.
This salt is not the same as ambrosia,
no matter how natural or obedient,
it's not sweet. I'm done being the witness,
the coffin and the collector. At long last
I'm in need of space. Skin is a popular
masterpiece, like clay living for my touch,
but my ledger is full.

THE WORK THAT CANNOT BE DONE ALONE

I'm so much happier
when I'm by myself. I can go
at least seven days without seeing
another human. I'm the hermit
in the desert, but I eventually ache
to show the sunrise to someone.
The work of love proves
that I'm more than a gritty animal.
I see the hole in my heart
fill with ash when you arrive,
a sign that I need to be held.
My brain cannot grow
without your eyes staring into mine.
I cannot be good without knowing
how to surrender, how to let you
be both a child and a man in my arms.
Relationships are a cosmic handout.
A challenge sits between me and my lover—
an infinity mirror that I can withstand
only because this person knows
when to cover my face.
Togetherness reveals a realm
as deep and hot as a volcano.
We'll burn up in there
if we do it right.

LAUREN SANDERSON

SOME OF THE
CHILDREN WERE
LISTENING

LAUREN
SANDERSON

BURIAL GROUND

The hills pull a sheet
across the faces of the dead.

Little heaps of secrets.
Pity the stars

that mistake us for stars.
I know more

than a galaxy
should.

I saw the sun
pull a knife on the dark,

pick the pockets
of a corpse.

It's no mortician.
Who wants to die

in the daylight?
Who wants to know

anything more?
I am trying to forget

this ancient way of burying
a man alive

but my pockets
are full of it.

SEEMA REZA

A
CONSTELLATION
of
HALF-LIVES

SEEMA REZA

BELEMNITE (I DREAM YOU ARE IN MY BED)

Disoriented by your smell
I can't remember your name
I dip my finger into the depression where
neck & shoulder & clavicle intersect
& ask, *Is it you? Are we here again?*

Never have the borders of my body been so blurred:
your flesh mine, my flesh yours.
The free exchange of fluids, the reckless drawing of blood:
There is no intimacy like a wrecking love.

Some nights I lay in (our) bed awake. These nights stretch.
I stand from the bed, sit on the toilet. Bore of masturbating.
Open & close books. Remove layers of blankets, layers of clothing.
Stand under the shower. Eat ripe fruit over the sink.
Wipe my face with a dishtowel.

These are my most honest nights.

Since the untangling the lovers have been kind & clumsy & graceful.
Hungry & apathetic. I couldn't say how many—it doesn't matter.
They are not enough.

Lately I prefer to find myself curled upright in the bathtub,
chin between the twin flats of my knees. When I am alone,
I am almost enough.

In daylight I face others propped upright, wounds dressed,
wrapped in hard plaster. Underneath the casing I am all hollow.
                    I think: *You are boring, boring, boring.*

I read many interesting things. I am so smart,
I read things most people wouldn't. While I read,
my mind wanders to fixate on men who think I'm great,
but not good enough. There are plenty of men like that
& they confirm what I recite in my head (in your voice):
                    not enough, not enough, not enough.

When I meet a man like that, the longing is unbearable.

The last time you were in this bed, it stood in the little house we bought.
We had given up, you were on edge, drinking too much,

pacing late into the night. I'd pack for my impending move,

go to work & come home to find my things unpacked.

It was like that for us:
You showed love through bared teeth. I offered sex as sedative.
That last night you woke me. Stood over me with a flashlight asking,
Are you okay? You were crying out in your sleep.

I lifted the covers, allowed you to lay beside me.
To fuck dangerous men to sleep is not unlike the circus trick
of putting one's head into a lion's gaping mouth. There's a certain
glamour & giddiness to escaping unscathed.

But I never cry out in my sleep.

When dreaming of my own death, I fall silent.

NOAH ARHM CHOI

FALL FOR HER

Fuck it. Fill your hands
with her though you tremble,
the daisy outside your door
stuck between bending
beneath the wind
and rising from the ground.

Fickle inheritance. You learned
the romance of being unseen. The moment
you should move from chair to under table,
just when your father turns away, just
before he picks up the hammer
and wonders where to throw.

When she looks at you,
holds out a hand, does she realize
what she is asking?
Does she see how deeply
your memories of him
wrap around your spine
with their greedy long limbs,
claiming tailbone, your tongue,
your skin too sweaty to grasp?

She is a bullet not meant to hurt you.
A bullet wanting to shine its face with your blood
in order to know what way you move. Intimacy
is its own kind of death; learning to say yes
to this ash to say enter
as easily as you say hide, how to still
while the bullet comes.

Fall or stay perched inside the small cage
of your teeth. Fall or agree to a life of being half,
never more than a hand
that knows to tighten in a fist
or unleash a string
and you've lost your chance to forget
you're the daughter
of a violent man.

FAREWELL, JACK

We all lose golden people. Sometimes it's a soft sadness and sometimes it's a forever hole inside you. Jack is the latter. When I started doing poetry, my only concern was me. Getting better. Getting my work out there more. Jack showed me that you can be a competitive person, full of love and giving and that it's good to look outward and remember people are hurting. They are fucking hurting. He made me remember that I could always be better. I chunk it and mess up sometimes. I say the wrong thing, joke too much, hurt someone's feelings and am still learning how to be a sweeter human. Jack seemed to be maxed on learning sweetness. I offered to buy a round every time I saw him at a bar and he always said, "Derrick. Half my poems are about being sober for over twenty-five years." He would smile and I'd feel real dumb and it was fine. When you look at your fellow writers in your community, look them in the eyes. Imagine them gone for good. It seems impossible. See them beyond being a writer, a weirdo, an entertainment source, an adversary, a competitor. They are a suffering jukebox (David Berman) and what a treat to spend a short time with them.

—DCB

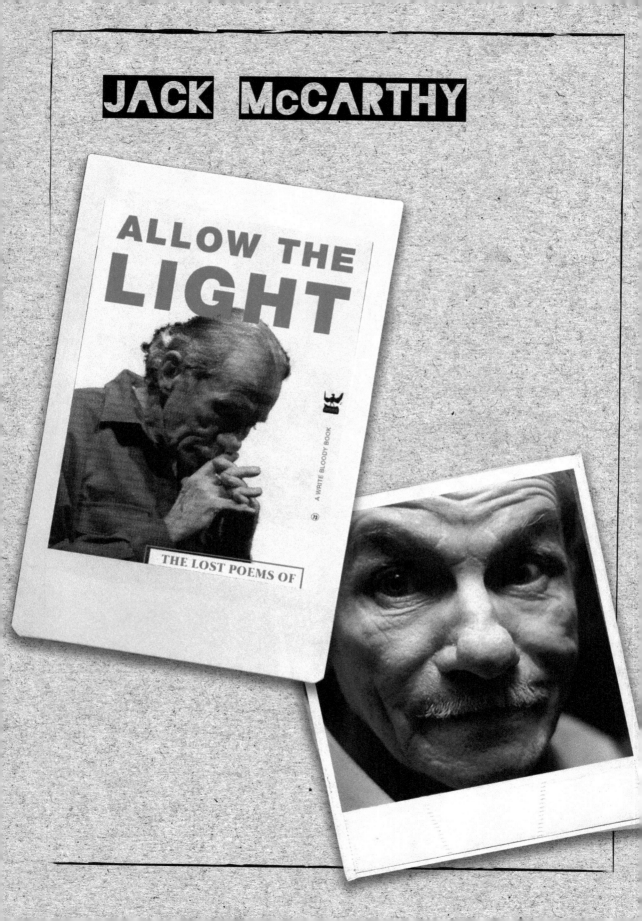

POSTER BOY

My mother was killed in a car accident
when I was seventeen and my father died
six months later of a broken heart
and I wasted no time becoming an alcoholic.

Five years later I was
in recovery from the alcoholism devoting all
of my attention
to healing that and it was as if
that other wound was
cauterized
with the white-hot branding iron
of the Double-A.

And in the years that followed
I knew that beneath the scar
of that searing
there was business that I needed to do, that
I would never be whole
unless I opened that up again.

But if I wasn't whole I was functional and if
I let those demons out
I wasn't sure they wouldn't
take me over.

So I settled and you'd think this story
wouldn't have a happy ending
but Surprise! now I believe
slow healing can happen
from the outside in
and for that principle I am the
poster-boy.

The only downside is
it took me forty years to get here.

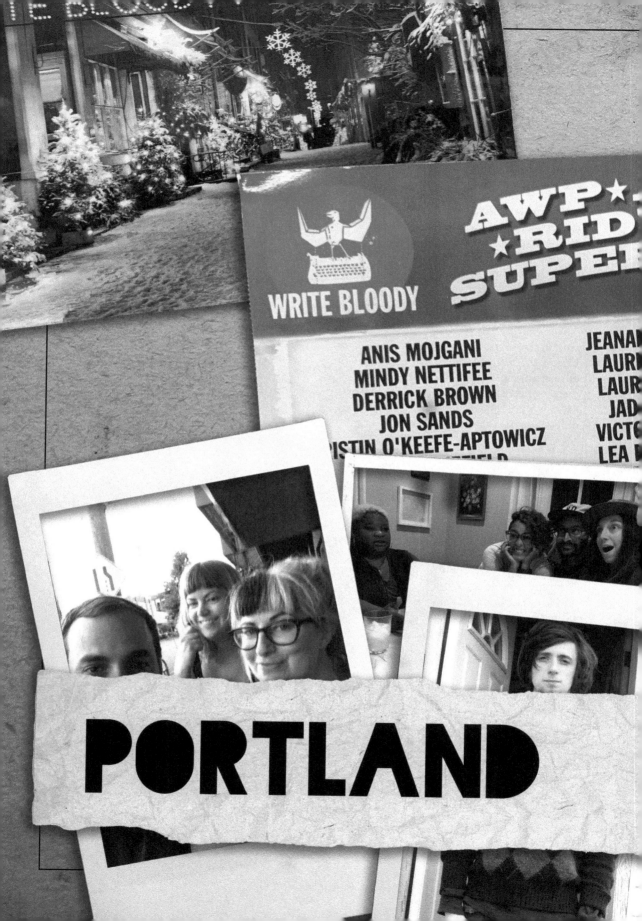

WRITE BLOODY

AWP★
★RID
SUPER

ANIS MOJGANI
MINDY NETTIFEE
DERRICK BROWN
JON SANDS
ISTIN O'KEEFE-APTOWICZ

JEANA
LAUR
LAUR
JAD
VICTO
LEA

PORTLAND

2020

This was a mistake. I did not feel like myself in Portland. I got real sad, on Wellbutrin and so much drinking and heartache. The weather sadness is so real. Don't let anyone fib on ya, it is eight months of gray and three months of purely magical weather. I love this comedy scene so much. The food world is off the charts. If you are a tenderoni, I cannot recommend enough to not try and endure Portland weather. It's a book lovers heaven. There are beautiful authors here doing cool shows like Jenna Fletcher, Matthew Dickman, Eryn Berg, Frayn Masters, Anis Mojgani, Stephen Meads, Brian Ellis, Mindy Nettifee, Annelyse Gelman and more, but I need more sun-magic and less heart static.

—DCB

THE FIREPLACE REACHES OUT TO ME

The fireplace looks like a wide-eyed Brahman bull
reaching for release from its tight cage

I reach toward it, warming my hands
teasing the flame

The pine cabin walls are terrified
We are drunk and loading more logs into the bull's mouth

Old age is upstairs
and the minibar is full of fast-forward buttons

A bobcat knocks on the door
and politely asks for my trash

I give him my dream journal
He is so grateful

A wall of books sits victorious and arrogant
If I could just get to a place where I am left in a dusty cabin for decor

She has passed out under an unspooky moon
I love her
She sleeps like an underpaid trucker
I love her
The clumsy pinecones plunk down on the tin, still fast asleep
I love her
The fire lurches toward her hair, it's fine
I love her
She is snoring and the trees are scared someone is sawing
I love her
The ashes of the fireplace ticker tape across the planks, I motorcade wave
I love her
The clouds of night keep blowing out the sky candles, relighting as they pass
I love her
We are soft, forgotten things in the middle of nowhere. Her dad is gone. I am
eavesdropping on her dreams, a blanket clumsy over her legs. Can we live here? The fire
is growing. We're on an inner tube in the snow and everyone we love is alive. Her legs
twitch, a beast in the fireplace learns to relax. She runs into a pageant of snowflakes; long
white runways await. She smiles into the couch, eyes closed, head warm.

I won.

We are made less terrible by each other.

12 STEP TRAINING MANUAL FOR THE CALL

1. When the phone rings, it will sound the same as any other call. Your reluctance to answer will tell you otherwise. Answer it anyway.

2. Sudden death is not quiet. Practice smashing dishes against the wall. Let the tea kettle scream. Start moaning *No* into the loud, guttural stillness.

3. Exercise your jaw. Open and close it while watching TV. When the call comes, the pain will need somewhere to go. Your jaw will thrust open against your will. Your mouth: the exit door.

4. Practice throwing yourself to your knees. Start somewhere soft like the carpet and work your way up to the hardwood floor where you keep your phone.

5. Get your affairs in order. Fill the gas tank, shower, eat three meals a day. This will prevent you from having to make any unnecessary stops on your way to console friends and family.

6. Padlock your liquor cabinet. Remember you come from generations of drinkers the length of a tightrope across the Atlantic and everyone falls in. Remind yourself that your brother wasn't a good swimmer and neither are you.

7. Set your alarm for various times in the night. Upon waking, you will have trouble distinguishing between your nightmares and reality. Whichever feels worse, that's reality.

8. Drive to your childhood home. The people inside will look like your parents but they will be cored like fruit. Their eyes, drained of color, will look straight through you. Seperate yourself.

9. If at all possible, go to the beach. Stand in the ocean and let the waves take you out. Do not resurface until you are sure you will drown. Repeat.

LOS ANGELES

2021-BEYOND

We're back here for now and it feels good, almost twenty years of doing this. We're still learning and growing. We may end up back in Long Beach, maybe NYC someday. Also. Nikki Steele has been an incredible genius champion of poetry for us. If ever near Boulder. Say yeehooo! I do have a dream of opening the Fascination Station Bookstore and Showcase someday. (Investors! Holler!) Here's some dream drawings of it done by Matt Bogart. Thank you to the authors who are road dogs every year, making poetry less dorky, revealing its power. Thank you to all the interns and advice heavers that have changed me and this odd path I am on forever. To those of you wanting to be published, you are a writer. There is no validation better than knowing something is finished. Your time is coming, you hot ass.

—DCB

JANAE JOHNSON

LESSONS
ON
BEING
TENDER
HEADED

HEADED

POEMS

JANAE JOHNSON

73

ANDRAGOGY OR; HOLD ME

If you hold me, let it be
like God holds the world.

Let your cheekbone graze the soil
of my chest. Slowly glide your palms

around my waist. Press your fingertips
into each splinter of skin & trust

neither of us will bleed tonight.
This is how you hold me.

    Have you ever listened
    to the heaving ribcage of a Black girl?

    Sounds like a sunken treasure chest.
    There's something holy about learning to swim

    for the sake of discovery.
    You find nothing is extinct.

    Blood is eternal when it surrenders to tides
    & gold is the least of her worth. Have you felt her skin?

    Isn't it selfless as a Sunday sunrise? Bones melting
    like lava returning to Earth's nest. Her uneven spine & bursting

    belly splitting the same heartbeat. You will hear
    languages she was never taught to speak

    or speak up to. She is pained but it is not your job
    to undo. Follow her breath as the first flicker of light.

    Do not assume any part of her has walked
    your earth before. Listen.

If there is ever a time to underestimate your strength,
it is when you decide to hold me.

    Have you ever lost yourself in the heaven
    of a Black girl's eyes?

    It is like watching an army
    of Gods carving a sunset.

    & have you ever kissed the bare back
    of a Black girl? It is like drinking

sugar out of a honey jar, lips tickled sweet.
Her shoulders bloom-sprouted wings

so celestial the act feels senseless,
like gravity teaching itself to stay

still. Ever felt her rage? Like a pendulum
injecting her forearms, swinging

her breath, coloring a charcoal sky.
Yes, that quickened thunderstorm you've seen

— mayhem, red-eyed temper— was never inside of her.
Can you not feel this now?

When you hold her, she is close-eyed brightness,
underground parachute, blanket-warm cotton

beneath a somersault. See? This molten-colored fury
was not inside of her, only the world trying to become her.

There is something too patient about the moon
& I never understood why we choose to sleep

when there is so much darkness to consume.
So fuel me in my unrest tonight & hold me

tight & willingly like God held the world, like rainfall
held the gossip of heaven, like the first time

you held your laughter, both hands locking your lips
& your lungs pulsing its rupture. Listen.

TICKET

the show ends but there's still a body
it is suggested they "make a puppet."

the corpse is distressed.
it has been a show for

a lifetime. its given its mobility
to the unknown

its audience. a journey
for everyone but

everyone wants more. soon
the hands are gathered

at the feet and the corpse
is tied to the living once again.

the corpse can't dance the
way it would without strings

but the corpse does dance
until it falls apart

again. the audience loses interest
and leaves the show behind. a corpse

and its marionette. died too
early for them

to make any real profit. from it
a person's leather wares thin

and the corpse becomes culture.
when the bones show

through its strings
it is still puppet

strung from a missing person
it becomes a sculpture.

feet made to stand upright
for a hundred years. the museum

gathers at the feet
until the glass separates the taxidermy from

the people. now
an exhibit. a ticket

longer than its ever been
a person.

JEFFREY McDANIEL

Thin Ice Olympics   Jeffrey McDaniel

THE VASE

My mother told me
that when she dies
she wants to be enrolled
in a furnace
and turned into ash,
then she wants me
to leave the ash outside
in a big glass bowl
and let the rain
soak into it,
then me to stir it up
into a kind of clay,
make a vase out of it,
put it in a kiln,
and when I die,
have my ashes
placed inside,
so she can carry me
again, forever.

KIMBERLY NGUYEN

HERE I AM
BURN ME

KIMBERLY NGUYEN

NGỦ NGÔN

what i thought i knew about language   i was wrong
forgive me: i once thought home would be
wherever my first language was   but the last night
i laid with you   we were two drops of water
under the blanket   of a dry, yearning tongue
when you asked me   how to say goodnight in vietnamese
i turned my whole body away   a syllable, misfired
into the dark   my first language—an arrow
that once grazed across my face   the sharp edge, leaving a laceration
that became my mouth.   i don't know how to speak
tenderness in my first language   i caught the arrow between my teeth
and now every utterance breaks skin   i know now
my second language is what saved me,   a salve for a split tongue
our first languages   are also sometimes our first wounds
my second language   warm honey on a cold, hard throat
the only language i can say   goodnight and i love you
the only language i could cry in   when you left me
but before that, in the chasm   between my back and your face,
you whispered the softest words   in mandarin—
your first language—   a voice i'll never hear again
i don't know what you said   and i will never need to know
while you slept, i lifted the words off your lips
on my tongue   all i could taste was their sweetness.

JOHN-FRANCIS QUIÑONEZ

73

John-Francis Quiñonez

KEEP YOUR LITTLE LIGHTS ALIVE

(Poems after Kate Bush's *Hounds of Love* and others)

I KNOW, IN SOME WAYS, I MUST BE ANSWERING FOR ALL THE TIMES I BEGGED FOR MORE TIME IN MY KITCHEN

When the sun peels from my living bones to reveal
a forever dark I've heard of - Dress me in lemon.

I am not let back to my home for a week
& my houseplants lean like ovened herbs in butter.
These times are loud-smell and out of breath leaning on my weak.

Where on the tongue does the will live?

I am trying to unstuck
sour candy from the gap in my teeth,
but all these moving parts grow wider.

Got the molar out Finally before it curled my skull into a hurt diamond.
Was in and out of the office in just an hour.
Time makes funny deposits like salt rings true in the maw.
What has flavor or weathering wrought
other than a hole in my mouth and born-debt?

I am worth 63 Whole American dollars, but
all I wanted was to be rich in hours.

Now I am hoarding groceries/
Pawing at lively shapes lest they bruise and ripple
in their own undoing - I can't blame them,
but I Bloat with these Gifts.

I do my best to get Full
three times daily.
Bless these segmented days. Cubed hours. Stolen watch-stock.

Is this what we meant when we asked for things to slow down for just a minute?
I've got questions at the business end of a 3 hour phone que.

Besides many things,
What does the knife do that
a reflection does not do to my sense of well being?

How can I brush my eye back into a tasteful shape or
Pour the warm of me into the Palm of my Bed
without Crying?

How does one plate a ghost for vespers?
What's a hymn but a course for reckoning? What oil is safe to wet my rosary
And if the people
    are hungry and looking in – what do I charge them?

Lord,
Sweet Lord,
    if this is life with all my prayers
                    Answered
                        then eat me.

COURTNEY LeBLANC

WHEN MY THERAPIST ASKS HOW I'M DOING

from *Her Whole Bright Life*

I talk about the election, my father's death, my friend's
brain tumor. I don't tell her about my two and a half
hour workout that morning, how I wouldn't stop until
I burned 1,000 calories. I don't tell her of my daily
ritual of stripping down, exhaling every ounce of breath
before stepping onto the scale. How if I have a hair tie
around my wrist it must be removed and the ritual
repeated. I don't tell her I know the calories of my
morning coffee (102) or my yogurt and granola (199)
or how I fear growing into my mother's body.
I spent a decade eating nothing more than an apple
and two rice cakes between the hours of 8 and 4.
When I gave up that slow march toward a hungry
death I thought I'd be normal. But what is normal
if not tracking every bite of broccoli? If not knowing
the calories in a single baby carrot (4). I don't tell
my therapist this because I like when my clavicles arch
out from my chest, when my hip bones jut forward
like handlebars. I don't tell her because I don't
want to talk about what ended fifteen years ago,
even if its fingerprints remain etched permanently
on me. Instead I talk about the daily hikes with my dog,
my friend's chemo regiment, the new meditation app
I downloaded. The session ends and I scoop up the
rumpled Kleenex and drop them in the garbage. There's
a bowl of leftover Halloween candy near the exit. I dig
for a Snickers, pop the bite-size chocolate into my mouth
and make it last until I reach my car. This time I don't
record it. This time, I regret not taking two.

LEXI PELLEGRINO

THRESHOLD

from *Let Go With The Lights On*

I learned the phrase *pubic hair* from my stepbrother.

We were in the garage, taking turns sticking our heads

in the freezer, and he had given me the last blue popsicle

because I had beaten him at Slaps three times.

He was smiling, braces shining like a silver medal

as he detailed slipping off my pajama pants at night

and staring at the shy cumulus curled between my legs,

that sparse field of prefix. He said *bush*

and I thought of what I used to hide behind as a child.

Though I was still young, I could sense the tender

threshold that marks the before and the after

the way feet find the deep end of the pool

before the rest of you dips under to catch up.

My child self stepping away from me into photos,

unable to wipe that stupid blue stain

from her lips. I thought about calling him a liar,

about screaming, ripping the flap of his sunburn down

until he was nothing, I thought about tattling,

spitting, waiting until his neck could be crushed

by the freezer door, I kissed him.

ANIS MOJGANI

GRATITUDE

from *After the Fire* and originally published in the *New York Times*

thankful for the bend
without the break

the branch beneath the weight of the finch
lightboned they be

the shake of a fir to alight a sky
for the earth

still having not released us
from their embrace

their rivers that peak
those stars

on clear nights
swimming through both

for the crows
consistent in their caw

as if saying *wake*
the morning lies in the street

wanting of me to be bronzed with its kiss
that every day in my city

the people strengthen together
for something unseen and powerful

for somewhere in the distance
the ocean calling

like an answer

lifting towards a grace
spoken for someone else

coming back to that which had tossed it
from where it had been thrown

ASHIA AJANI

PORCH

from *Heirloom*

"I keep a shotgun in every corner of my bedroom,
and the first cracker even looks like he wants to throw
some dynamite on my porch, won't write his mama again."

—Fannie Lou Hamer

I keep a piece of myself on the porch.
Don't test me. I have had everything ripped from my flesh
and still fix my gums to smile at those who wish me harm.
don't try it. I am a nigga who comes from niggas and as such
I do not play. This body owns nothing- exists everywhere. You
can't kill me. All the fullness in the world collides within my frame.
A grand unraveling weathers me mighty vengeful: can you say the same? My love
shatters anything that has tried to cause me harm. Ceremony predates
survival, so leave my flowers at the doorstep and dance until your
heart bursts into a thousand new iterations of Godliness. Fill my cup
with lilac wine where one can pull a Nina croon through
the window until a swansong of rage fills the walls and covers me
in honeysuckle rose. Give me all that I desire or nothing at all.
I want a new wig. I want a plot of land. I want a small win
that carries me through the rest of forever.
I am owed at least that.

DERRICK C. BROWN

PHLOX

from *Love Ends In A Tandem Kayak*

The summer of wallow too hard.
The summer of Finched color.
Sidewalk drunks assassinated my Birds of Paradise.
We should still be together.

I deserve every morsel of paranoia.
The night is still hunting me.
Does this jacket make me look like an exit?
We could still have the child.

You summoned me
like I could skip the line at the fair
for watermelon summer.
We could be one admission apart.

You reached into the rind with a lead fist
and pulled out the center
and my heart stopped.
We could have better lives.

You crammed it in my mouth, and my heart,
beat again.
Magical animal.
We could resurrect the fleet of desire.

Pulp gulp. Grandeur
dripping down my face like a teen pink sunset.
Your godless face, your gift to my puzzle.
We could be in pillows.

My tears flow
for some dog
to come and taste.
We could try and try after trying.

You forgive me, and Death Valley
is blown from every map.
We could wander and end.

You forgave me.
Arms full of Phlox,
and I vomited monarchs.
We both hear children scream in the park,
not sure if it's joy.

Poems by Karen Finneyfrock

Illustrated poems to seduce and destroy
EDITED BY DERRICK BROWN

RAYON HAUS
I LOVE YOU IS BAC
DERRICK C. BROWN

ORN IN THE YEAR OF
HE BUTTERFLY KNIFE
a Write Bloody Book

COLLECTED UNDERGROUND WRITINGS (1993-2008) OF DERRICK C. BROWN
NATIONAL BESTSELLER

73

Favorite Daughter
Nancy Huang
A WRITE BLOODY BOOK   15.00

Cast Your Eyes
Like Riverstones Into
The Exquisite Dark
a write bloody boo

A Book Of Night Poe
Danny She

POLE DANCING
TO
OSPEL HYMNS

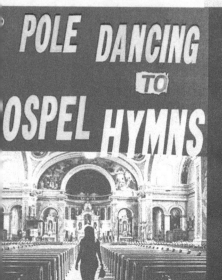

ELAINA M. ELLIS
**WRITE
ABOUT AN
EMPTY
BIRDCAGE**
a Write Bloody Book
73
15.00

a Write Bloody Book

Rise of the Trust Fal
Mindy Nettifee

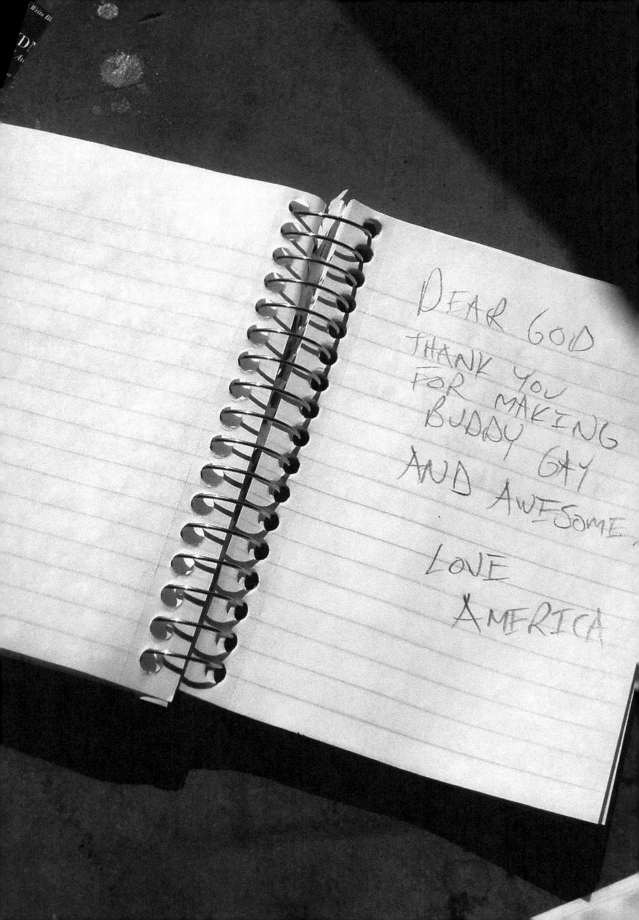

ACKNOWLEDGMENTS

So many people helped me when I was busted up and downhearted. Diana Barrie Shattuck set up the opera house shows and housed us all, Aly Sarafa worked overtime, Daniel Lisi kept us organized, SCB distributors: John, Gabe, Aaaron, took a huge chance on us, WB UK and WB North inspire me, Amber Tamblyn helped us get distribution, Mindy Nettifee brought me hard-boiled eggs when I couldn't afford food, Katie Hogan, Amy Saul Zerby and Keaton Maddox kept my spirits up, Jessica Abughattas worked in the blazing hot office without any complaints, Jene "Gootz" worked the bookstore when I felt burnt out, Bucky Sinister and Beau Sia stood by my bedside at the hospital, Buddy Wakefield drove across the country with me a billion times, Andrea Gibson and Megan Falley sometimes call so I can make them laugh… Just a butt load of designers who didn't get paid enough, promoters who took a chance, poets who loaned their couches and beer, interns who deserved the world and knew we were low budge, I am humbled as all hell and grateful in my bones for the help and time and caring for me and the press. All I want is for there to be more poetry in the world that does what poetry is meant to do. To do it's quiet magic and ruin others the lovely way it has ruined me.

—DCB

PS. We collected from tons of folks tons of photos they had on their phones. We realized late that the task of hunting all the photographers and cover designers was monumental. If we missed you, we will post on our sites and ebooks. Just DM us and let us know which photo.

Thanks to: Maust, Noyel Gallimore, Amy Marie Photography, Red Rabbit Shoots Color, and to every photographer and designer who ever shared their spirit and skill with us.

Franny Choi author photo by Francesca B. Marie

Jeffrey McDaniel author photo by Caroline Kaye

Derrick C. Brown author photo by Noyel Gallimore

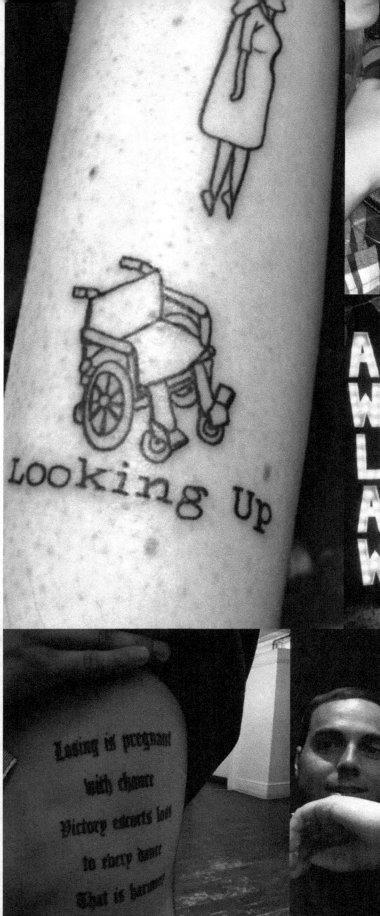

Looking up

love is yours

A STORY OF
WILD ME
LOST
AMONG
WILD YOU

Losing is pregnant
with chance
Victory escorts loss
to every dance
That is become

Today is the day
we must come alive

WRITE BLOODY BOOKS

After the Fire — Anis Morgani

After the Witch Hunt — Megan Falley

Aim for the Head: An Anthology of Zombie Poetry — Rob Sturma, Editor

Allow The Light: The Lost Poems of Jack McCarthy — Jessica Lohafer, Editor

Amulet — Jason Bayani

Any Psalm You Want — Khary Jackson

Atrophy — Jackson Burgess

Birthday Girl with Possum — Brendan Constantine

The Bones Below — Sierra DeMulder

Born in the Year of the Butterfly Knife — Derrick C. Brown

Bouquet of Red Flags — Taylor Mali

Bring Down the Chandeliers — Tara Hardy

Ceremony for the Choking Ghost — Karen Finneyfrock

A Constellation of Half-Lives — Seema Reza

Counting Descent — Clint Smith

Courage: Daring Poems for Gutsy Girls — Karen Finneyfrock, Mindy Nettifee, & Rachel McKibbens, Editors

Cut to Bloom — Arhm Choi Wild

Dear Future Boyfriend — Cristin O'Keefe Aptowicz

Do Not Bring Him Water — Caitlin Scarano

Don't Smell the Floss — Matty Byloos

Drive Here and Devastate Me — Megan Falley

Drunks and Other Poems of Recovery — Jack McCarthy

The Elephant Engine High Dive Revival — Derrick C. Brown, Editor

Every Little Vanishing — Sheleen McElhinney

Everyone I Love Is a Stranger to Someone — Annelyse Gelman

Everything Is Everything — Cristin O'Keefe Aptowicz

Favorite Daughter — Nancy Huang

The Feather Room — Anis Mojgani

Floating, Brilliant, Gone — Franny Choi

Glitter in the Blood: A Poet's Manifesto for Better, Braver Writing — Mindy Nettifee

Gold That Frames the Mirror — Brandon Melendez

The Heart of a Comet — Pages D. Matam

Heavy Lead Birdsong — Ryler Dustin

Heirloom — Ashia Ajani

Hello. It Doesn't Matter. — Derrick C. Brown

TOUR BUDS FOREVER, JOEL C

SAUL WILLIAMS

COLD WAR KIDS TOUR

poetry and rock and roll

OPEN BOOKS

the king, Beau Sia

JESUS IS LORD

DO YOU PARTY?

Love you J Mack

CPSIA information can be obtained
at www.ICGtesting.com
Printed in the USA
BVHW010904160922
646936BV00001BA/1

9 781949 342352